The Water of Life

By
George Edward Fifield, D.D.

Author of
"God is Love"

Patrick Irving, 2025

Copyright © 2026, George Edward Fifield, D.D.

All rights reserved. The moral right of the editor has been asserted.

Transcribed from an original printing of The Water of Life by George Fifield (The Recorder Press).

This modern edition was prepared from a personal copy of the original text and formatted for clarity and accessibility.

This edition of The Water of Life by George Fifield is a faithful word-for-word transcription of the original text published circa 1927 by The Recorder Press in Plainfield, New Jersey. Spelling, punctuation, and capitalization have been preserved as printed, except where clear typographical errors have been silently corrected. Italics and emphasis follow the original. Additions made by the editor appear in italicized parentheses to distinguish them from the author's original text. The goal of this edition is to make Fifield's Christ-centered message available to a new generation of readers while maintaining the integrity of his original thought and expression.

All rights to this transcription © 2025 Patrick Irving.

The original text is in the public domain.

This book and all other publications are available for free at maranathamedia.com. To order additional copies, please contact us at fatheroflovefellowship@gmail.com.

ISBN: 979-8-9948137-0-6 (paperback)
ISBN: 979-8-9948137-1-3 (ebook)

Published in Harrodsburg, Kentucky

"For whosoever will save his life shall lose it; and whosoever will lose his life for my sake shall find it."—Matthew 16:25

Originally published by The Recorder Press, circa 1927

This modern reprint edition was edited and prepared by Patrick Irving, in collaboration with Adrian Ebens and Father of Love Fellowship.

Foreword

This rediscovery of *The Water of Life* by George E. Fifield is more than the recovery of a forgotten book—it is the revival of a voice that once bore clear witness to the gospel in its simplest and most beautiful form. In an age when theological discourse often drifts toward abstraction, Fifield's words draw the reader back to the living heart of righteousness by faith—that "most precious message" entrusted to God's people more than a century ago.

My first encounter with Fifield came through his better-known volume, *God Is Love* (1897). Few books have so profoundly shaped my understanding of the gospel. Its portrayal of divine justice and mercy as coextensive expressions of the same eternal love was, to me, nothing short of transformative. Rarely have I encountered a presentation of righteousness by faith so unadorned in form, yet so exquisite in its theological depth and spiritual beauty. It unveiled a vision of God wholly consistent with the nonviolent character of the One we call our Savior: not a deity requiring sacrifice or penal satisfaction, but a Father whose justice is restorative, and whose supreme purpose is the reconciliation and healing of His children from the disease of sin.

When *The Water of Life* surfaced—an almost unknown companion to *God Is Love*—it was as though an unfinished melody had found its closing refrain. It bears no publication date, yet a dedication note included in the first few pages of the volume attests to its posthumous publication by Fifield's wife, circa 1927, as a memorial edition issued by The Recorder Press—a Seventh Day Baptist publishing house. Though published outside denominational channels, this volume breathes the same spirit as that proclaimed by the forerunners of the message of righteousness by faith.

That a work so rich in spiritual insight and so clearly rooted in the theological current of 1888 should have lain dormant for generations is, in my view, a most remarkable occurrence. Only a handful of copies are known to exist today, and its near extinction has rendered it virtually invisible to modern readers. Yet its message, like the living water of which it speaks, has lost none of its vitality.

Fifield stands among those early Adventist thinkers most deeply influenced by the 1888 message of righteousness by faith. Alongside E. J. Waggoner and A. T. Jones, he recognized that the gospel is not a legal transaction to adjust God's attitude toward humanity, but a healing revelation that restores the human heart to harmony with the divine character. In *The Water of Life*, this theme reaches a serene maturity. Sin is portrayed not as the violation of an arbitrary decree, but as separation from the Source of life itself; and salvation, not as judicial pardon alone, but as the restoration of union with Christ—the living channel of divine love.

That this book should have lain in obscurity for nearly a century is both tragic and providential. Tragic, because a message so pure and Christ-centered was nearly silenced; providential, because it now reappears at a time when the world once more thirsts for the reality of a God who is wholly good. For those within Adventism still seeking to grasp the depth of the 1888 message, this little volume offers a window into how that light was once received and cherished.

The Water of Life is not merely a historical artifact—it is a living testimony. Its pages breathe the quiet assurance that the love of God is the very law of life in the universe. To read Fifield is to witness the enduring thread of God's everlasting gospel: the covenant of divine love spoken through the prophets, made manifest in Christ, and faithfully reflected in the message given at Minneapolis.

It is a rare privilege to see, after so many years, the spiritual insights of George Fifield restored to the public mind. His vision of divine love remains, in my opinion, among the purest expressions of the gospel ever written. If this edition helps renew interest in that message—and leads readers to the Christ whom Fifield so tenderly portrayed—its purpose will be fulfilled.

It is my prayer that this rediscovered work will foster a living appreciation for the theology of righteousness by faith as understood by some of our early pioneers, and that it will inspire readers to study more deeply the character of God as revealed in Jesus Christ. May the Spirit that once moved upon the hearts of those who heard and embraced the 1888 message move again through these pages.

— Patrick Irving
Author of *Behold the Lamb:
A Treatise on the Character of God*

Introduction

What a joy to receive this treasure of a book and find in it so many points that confirm the light that has come to the Father of Love Movement. We have been blessed by Fifield's 1897 sermons with its beautiful study from Isaiah 53 exposing pagan conceptions of appeasement. We have read his book *God Is Love* and rejoiced in his beautiful definition of the atonement and the embryonic thoughts on the true character of God.

In this volume, released after his death, we see the capstone of Fifield's thoughts. One might think that by the 1920's Fifield might have been affected by the doctrinal causalities of many of the men around him, but none of this is present in this volume.

We see the Father and Son relationship clearly defined along the lines of what Ellen White describes in *Desire of Ages* page 21 as the circuit of beneficence. The Holy Spirit is presented as the omnipresence of the Father and Son who make their abode with us.

All the 1888 principles of the present Cross and the covenants, and the principles of righteousness by faith bubble forth from the beautiful expressions of each chapter. Fifield exposes the false view of the atonement of appeasement through literal blood, and the arbitrary nature of Christianity's God. The beautiful theme of the fountain described in Revelation that brings life wherever it goes is described with simplicity yet clarity.

The theme of Waggoner presenting the blood of Christ as his life are repeated and expanded by Fifield who shows that the blood is the omnipresent Spirit of the Father and the Son. He goes on to make the beautiful point that in 1 John 5:8 the Spirit, the water and the blood all agree in one. Water and Spirit are both symbols of life and therefore so must the blood. For blood to agree with water and Spirit, it must speak of life not death.

The book draws out all the riches of Adventism with a beautiful journey into the Sanctuary and its application to the gospel. Fifield then contrasts the beauty of the 1888 message with the philosophies of this world, showing his depth of understanding and application.

Truly this little volume is a masterpiece and must certainly fill its place as one of the key books of the Father of Love Movement.

It is a joy to be able to see the later fruit of what Fifield taught in the later 1890's. Fascinating that this book has been hidden away for almost 100 years, but now its time has come to play its part in completing the Fourth Angel's message.

We thank you Lord Jesus for bringing this precious book to our attention at this time through your son Patrick, and providentially kept in Australia until the time it was needed.

In faith, hope, and love,
—Adrian Ebens
November 2025

Note on the Discovery of this Text

In late 2025, a modest and poorly described online listing led to an unexpected find: an original copy of George Fifield's *The Water of Life*. At first glance, it appeared to be one of many forgotten devotional works from the early twentieth century. Yet upon examination, it became clear that this was something far rarer—a published book by a man whose name, though known among Adventist historians and students of the 1888 message, had almost vanished from print beyond his better-known *God Is Love* (1897).

Further investigation revealed that *The Water of Life* is almost entirely absent from public awareness. No digital copies exist, no modern reprints have been issued, and no contemporary Adventist publications even mention its title. Only a few known surviving copies appear in scattered library records—one held by Andrews University, and another in an archival collection in the UK—yet these remain effectively inaccessible to the wider public. Thus, although technically preserved, the book has been lost to living memory for almost a century.

Part of this obscurity may be due to the circumstances of its publication. Issued posthumously as a memorial edition by Fifield's wife, the volume was likely produced in a limited print run—intended primarily for family, friends, and perhaps a few ministerial colleagues. Without the author's oversight or denominational promotion, *The Water of Life* quietly faded into obscurity soon after its release.

For this reason, the present edition may rightly be called a rediscovery. It does not claim novelty of existence, but renewal of attention—a restoration of a voice long silent. Fifield's theology, deeply rooted in the revelation of God's love as seen in Jesus Christ, resonates powerfully with the 1888 message and with the broader Adventist struggle to understand divine justice, mercy, and character. To bring this forgotten work back into the light is not merely an act of antiquarian recovery, but an invitation to once again hear a message that may still speak to the heart of Adventism today.

An Explanation

This book was in process of preparation by my husband but was not completed on account of his death. The indulgence of the reader is asked for all that is lacking in the compilation and finish that his own hand would have supplied. It is now published as a memorial to him.

A.W.F.

To the friends who accepted and loved this everlasting Gospel, through the author's ministrations; and to the many readers, yet unknown, who may be blest thereby, this book is lovingly dedicated.

Preface

The water of life is the everlasting Gospel, the eternal, unchanging, outreaching, outflowing heart of Infinite Love, manifested through the Christ who is "the same yesterday, today and forever," to redeem each soul, and bring it back into fellowship and oneness with God.

Different ways of revealing this eternal truth there have been, through the Smitten Rock, through the Sacrifices, through the Sanctuary; and, when lost out of all these so that only a formal, lifeless ceremonialism remained, then, last of all, through the incarnation, life and death of Jesus, the Christ.

But whatever and however revealed, the truth itself and the working of this divine, outreaching power and life, in its effort to redeem and regenerate the sin-sick soul of man, is ever precisely the same in all ages and in all lands. This does not mean that God, who is infinite in loving resources, does not adapt the revelation and manifestation of this power to the varying understandings and needs of men of different concepts and different civilizations.

The object of this book is to set forth this everlasting Gospel of the pure outflowing river of the water of life, free from all human limitations of creeds, and from all the corruptions and superstitions of paganism.

Humbly do we implore and simply do we trust that Our Father will, through these pages here yielded up to Him, make this living water flow pure and free that it may be in us a well of water springing up into everlasting life.

The Author.

Contents

Foreword... v
Introduction... ix
Note on the Discovery of this Text xi
An Explanation xiii
Preface... xvii

I. The Water of Life 1
II. The River of Life 11
III. The Christian a Source of Water...................... 23
IV. The Tree of Life 37
V. Unity of Life.. 51
VI. Fellowship of Life 63
VII. The Cleansing Blood of Christ 73
VIII The Blood Is the Life............................... 83
IX The Symbol of the Blood.............................. 93
X Two Kinds of Righteousness 103
XI The Change of Raiment............................... 113
XII The Breastplate of Righteousness.................... 121
XIII Fullness of Life in Christ 131

*"Eternal depths of Love Divine,
In Jesus, God with us, displayed,
How bright Thy beaming glories shine
How wide Thy healing streams are spread."*

I

The Water of Life

"Whosoever drinketh of the water that I shall give him shall never thirst; but the water that I shall give him shall be in him a well of water springing up into everlasting life." —John 4:14.

1
The Water of Life

DID YOU ever think that the literal water is the **water of life?** Try to think the water out of the world, and ask yourself what you would have left. You can not grow one blade of grass without water; the entire vegetable kingdom is dependent upon water; and the animal kingdom depends upon the vegetable kingdom for sustenance. Without water not one particle of verdure, or of bloom or fruitage, would exist; the earth would be a dead, rolling mineral orb. The water **is** the water of life.

Now just what the water is to the physical world, God, through Christ, by His Spirit, is to the spiritual world. Without Christ, **the present Christ,** the world would be a moral desert, not one touch of spiritual bloom or beauty, or fragrance, or fruitage. This is not the theological dogma of total depravity. It is only saying that without the omnipresent Christ Spirit, the world would have been utterly depraved and lost, and even depopulated long ago by the curse of its own sin.

Even now it often seems to us that wrong is triumphant, robed and crowned and garlanded, while Truth and Right are ignominiously crucified. But what we now see in this world is not the result of evil free to do its worst. It is, so to speak, the overflow, after God, by His omnipresent restraining Spirit, has held back the swelling turbulent flood.

Had it not been true from the beginning that God, through the already given Christ, by the omnipresent Holy Spirit, had been seeking to make His voice heard in every soul, saying, "This is the Way, walk ye in it," man would soon have wholly given himself over to the cumulative power of evil. This being true, all of the spiritual life, and all of the unselfish love in the world, is the result of Christ, the living water.

You say, you have known people who loved unselfishly, and made heroic sacrifices before they were converted, or born again. "Christ is the Light that lighteth **every man** that cometh into the world." The living water comes into our lives in various ways: through a Christian heredity and a Christian environment. It is this Christ within that brings us to repentance, and to conscious submission to Himself, so making the new birth possible. It is of this light that Jesus spake when He said, "If therefore the light that is in thee be darkness, how great is that darkness!"[1] But however goodness may come into our lives, it is all the living water without which there could be **no spiritual life,** just as there could not be any animal or vegetable life without the physical water.

What is it, then, to confess Christ? Many think that to confess the Lord is simply to testify in some meeting, but this is only a small part of confessing Christ. To confess Christ is first to know and to realize the above truth of the living water, and then ever to acknowledge it, not only to others; but it is even of more importance that we always acknowledge it to ourselves. "Not unto us, O Lord, **not unto us,** but to Thy name give glory. For I know that **in me,** that is, in my flesh,

---

1 Matthew 6:23.

dwelleth no good thing." To know this, and ever to say it, is but to "Give unto the Lord the glory due unto His name."

Suppose I am an artist, and my home is decorated with pictures of my own painting. But my friend is a better artist than I am, and he has given me one of his masterpieces, which I have hung among my own pictures. You come to see me and admire the pictures very much, and I tell you, truly, that I painted them. After admiring many of my pictures we come to the picture my friend painted. You stand before it spellbound, and finally say, "I think this is the most beautiful of all." I do not say a word. I have denied my friend, when I ought to have confessed him. You do not have to say one word to deny Christ. You can deny and crucify Him even by your silence.

This is why it is so important always to confess Christ, even to ourselves. God is infinite fullness of power and beauty and blessing, and **there are no limitations on His part.** All that He is, and all that He has, He desires to impart to us and will do it as fast as we are able to receive it. But while we refuse to confess Christ, and take unto ourselves the glory of what He does for us, we defeat His work in us, and compel Him to hold His hand, else we would become **self-righteous** instead of righteous. When we fully and always confess Christ, we remove the limitations, which are all on **our part,** so God can work in us all the loving desires of His heart. O friends, let us always confess the Lord and not, like Peter, deny Him.

THE CIRCUIT OF THE WATERS

In nature, the ocean is the great fountain of life. All the streams rise in the ocean. The wandering winds bathe their wings in the sea then fly over the land giving showers of blessings. The primary circuit of the waters is from the ocean to the clouds, and the clouds to the earth, and the earth, through a thousand streams, back to the ocean again. Just as all the rivers rise in the ocean, so all flow into it completing the circuit. Were it not for this fact, the ocean itself would run dry and the earth become a desert.

So in the spiritual world, the river of life flows from the throne of God. The Psalmist says of God, "With Thee is the fountain of life." Even Christ is never spoken of as the ultimate source in distinction from God. Now, as of old, we may hear Him say, "I can of mine own self do nothing;" the "Father that dwelleth in me, He doeth the works." **All things are of God,** who is in Christ, reconciling the world unto Himself. As we have seen, the gift of the Holy Spirit was in the gift of the Son, and Christ Himself is but the outreaching heart of the Father. The primary circuit of blessing is from God, through Christ, by the Spirit, to the human soul; and from the human soul, in prayer and praise and thanksgiving, back to God.

We always desire to be very reverent in speaking of God. He is infinite and we are but finite. In the very nature of things we can never fully comprehend Him, but there are scriptures that seem to indicate that here as in the physical world, if the circuit were not completed, if the outflowing heart of the Infinite brought no returning flow of joyous praise and thanksgiving, the very Fountain of Life, the heart of God, would run dry. If this is so, we can understand why the Bible ever presents praise and thanksgiving as such an essential part of worship.

But in nature there is also a secondary circuit of the waters. You have heard that the cutting down of the forests will diminish the rainfall. And why? It is because trees facilitate the exchange of moisture. The roots of a tree reach down deep into the moist earth. They subdivide into millions of little rootlets and the end of each rootlet is a living sponge to absorb moisture and pass it along through the roots and up through the body of the tree out into the leaves. The leaves will wither quickly on a very warm day if the branch that bears them is cut off from the tree. It is because the water evaporates from them; but the water does not evaporate any faster after the branch is cut off than it did before. The supply has been cut off so the branch goes dry.

A large tree will take up immense quantities of water each day and throw it off into the air to come down again in local showers. The secondary circuit of the waters is thus from the earth to the tree, from the tree to the clouds, and from the clouds back to the earth again. All the water, it is true, comes from the ocean, through the primary circuit, but, were it not for the secondary circuit, after having been used only once, it would flow back to the ocean again. Through this secondary circuit it is used over and over; each time coming down in showers of blessings.

"A nice little study," we hear you say, "into the sources of the rainfall; but why is it given here?" It is because there is a secondary circuit in the spiritual world also. Of the righteous it is said, **"Trees of Righteousness** they shall be called, the planting of the Lord, that He may be glorified."[2] Where there is an assembly of Christians you have a grove of these trees of righteousness.

Now, you have seen Christians who are satisfied if they can go to church every Sabbath, or to a revival service, but if, for any reason, they are denied these privileges, they backslide. What is the trouble with them? It is that they do not know God for themselves. They have a churchly experience. They are dependent for their blessings entirely upon others. They are only in the secondary circuit.

Do not misunderstand me. It is not wrong to receive blessings from each other and enjoy them. He who is in the primary circuit and who knows God for Himself, will enjoy these local showers of blessing even more than any one else; but **he is not dependent upon them.** He can go out into the desert and waste places of life, and take

---

2   Isaiah 61:3.

God with him. It is all right to receive the witness of men, but, "If we receive the witness of men, the witness of God is greater, for he that hath the witness of God **hath the witness in himself."** Dear friends, do you **know** that God is **teaching you** and that **He** is **leading you** day by day? Or are you only taught by others who know God? Thank God for the primary circuit. Praise Him for the inexhaustible fountain. "Whosoever will, let him come and take of this water of life freely."

*"Immortal Love, for ever full,
For ever flowing free,
For ever shared, for ever whole,
A never-ebbing sea."*

II

The River of Life

"They shall be abundantly satisfied with the fatness of Thy house; and Thou shalt make them drink of the river of Thy pleasures.

"For with Thee is the fountain of life; in Thy light shall we see light."—Psalm 36:8,9.

"And he showed me a pure river of water of life clear as crystal, proceeding out of the throne of God and of the Lamb."—Revelation 22:1.

11
The River of Life

MANY HAVE only thought of this river of life as of a stream of literal water flowing from the throne through the fair fields of the Paradise of God. Thinking of it only thus, they have placed the enjoyment of it in the great hereafter and never dreamed of it as referring to this life.

We are not of those who think that the home of the saved is a mythical country or an unreal or imaginary land. We believe in a real life and a real home hereafter. We have no argument, therefore, with those who believe in the literal river of life in the literal Paradise of God; for we rejoice in that belief ourselves.

The Bible was written for the here; we shall not need it in the hereafter for there will then be different means of communication with God. It is here that "we know in part, and we prophesy in part. But when that which is perfect is come, then that which is in part shall be done away."[3] The promises of God, like Himself, are eternal; but, if we accept them by faith, they begin for us here and now. The

---

3   1 Cor. 13:9,10.

literal river will not mean less to us in the future, but rather infinitely more, by having experienced its spiritual significance here.

That it does have such for us now, if we grasp it, is plainly stated in the same chapter of Revelation, and seventeenth verse, that pictures this river flowing from the throne of God.

"And the Spirit and the Bride say, Come. And let him that heareth say, Come. And let him that is athirst, Come. And whosoever will, let him **take the water of life freely.**"[4]

Hundreds of years ago, the same invitation was given by Isaiah. "Ho every one that thirsteth, come ye to the waters; and he that hath no money; come ye."[5]

This river then has been flowing and freely flowing from the days of old. We have a right, therefore, to ask, what is its spiritual meaning for us now?

"In the last day, that great day of the feast, Jesus stood and cried saying, If any man thirst, let him come unto me and drink. He that believeth on me, as the scripture hath said, out of him shall flow rivers of living water. But this spake He of the Spirit, which they that believe on Him should receive."[6] Here the "living water" or "water of life" is plainly a symbol of the given Spirit or life of God. This figure of the water as a symbol of the Spirit goes through the whole Bible. The Lord by the prophet Joel says: "I will **pour out** my Spirit upon all flesh."

Pentecost is called the "early rain," and the final outpouring of the Spirit is called the "latter rain." These are the "waters of Shiloah that go softly;" and men refuse them, preferring the overflowing torrents of human numbers and power.

---

4   Rev. 22:17.
5   Isaiah 55:1.
6   John 7:37,38.

When the soldier pierced the side of the crucified and dying Christ, there came from that side two streams, one of blood and one of water. John tells us what these two streams signify:

"There are three who bear witness, the Spirit, and the water, and the blood; and these three agree in one."[7] It is clear that the "one" in which all three agree, is the Spirit. This is the divinely inspired statement that both the flowing "water of life," and the flowing blood, "which is the life," are symbols and representations of the outflowing Spirit or life of God, given us through Christ, His only begotten Son. The water of life is flowing for us now in a wondrous river from the throne of God. May He help us to understand that we may truly partake of its waters, for here **is** the **real** "Fountain of Life."

In that age of symbols, when God was teaching His people by kindergarten methods, Moses smote the Rock, and the water gushed out into the desert bringing with it verdure, and life, and joy. Speaking of this, Paul tells us that they "did all eat the same spiritual meat; and did all drink the same spiritual drink; for they drank of that spiritual Rock that followed them, and that Rock was Christ."[8]

Christ is the "Lamb slain from the foundation of the world."[9] It was in the beginning, then, that the real Rock was smitten, the Rock of which the rock in the wilderness was the symbol and the revelation. Here, again, as all through the Bible, the water is a symbol of the Spirit. The gift of the Spirit was in the gift of the Son. "He that spared not His own Son… how shall He not with Him also freely give us all things?"[10]

The scriptures plainly teach that in this Spirit of God outflowing from God, through Christ, is all creative, redemptive, and regenerative power. It is by this Spirit striving in human hearts that men are

---

7   1 John 5:8. Revised Version.
8   1 Cor. 10:3,4.
9   Rev. 13:8.
10 Romans 8:32.

brought to repentance, that by it also they may be forgiven, saved, sanctified, and glorified. The Spirit represents the personal presence of the Father and the Son, for it is by the Spirit that the promise to the believer is fulfilled: "We will come and make our abode with him."

Ever since Christ was given at the foundation of the world, this river of spiritual presence and of spiritual life, and of spiritual power, has been flowing from the throne of God. The heart of Infinite Love has been reaching out, through Christ, by the Holy Spirit, after every lost and wandering soul, the living water has come so near each one that "Whosoever will may take thereof and live."

Salvation is an omnipresent and a **present** spiritual, transforming power and life, to come **into** you **right now,** and **here,** and save you from your sins. And this power, and life, is the Spirit of God through Christ. Some may object that the Spirit was not given until Pentecost, quoting the following scripture:

"The Holy Ghost was not yet given, because that Jesus was not yet glorified." This scripture and others like it, do not mean what it has been made to mean in many sermons and in theological writings. It does not mean that the Spirit had not been given to the world. It simply means what it says: that the Spirit had not yet been given to the disciples, nor could He be given to them; for they could not reach a place in their experience where they were fitted to receive the Spirit while Jesus was with them. There was much of selfishness in their choice, when they left the fishermen's nets, and the receipt of custom, to follow Jesus.

They thought He soon would be crowned King in Jerusalem; and if they were the first to follow Him, they would have the chief places in the new Kingdom to be. They often disputed among themselves who of the twelve should have the chief places. Jesus told them plainly that He was to be killed instead of crowned, but they refused to believe it. Even after the resurrection, one of the first questions was, "Lord, wilt thou at **this time** restore the kingdom to Israel?" It was only when Jesus was crucified, risen, and ascended to Heaven, and every earthly hope of honor and earthly power was crucified with Him, and they realized that if they preached Christ at all, they must incur the scorn and persecution of the world by preaching a Saviour that was crucified instead of crowned, then self died in them utterly and they were ready for the outpouring of the Spirit.

But the Spirit had been given to the world ever since the gift of Christ at the beginning. Stephen knew this when he said to the Jews who were about to stone him: "Ye do always resist the Holy Ghost, **as your fathers did,** so do ye. Which of the prophets have not your fathers persecuted? And they have slain them which showed before the coming of the Just One, of whom ye have now been the betrayers, and murderers."

Clearly, in all this wickedness, the fathers were resisting the Holy Spirit. Before the flood, the Lord said, "My Spirit shall not **always strive with man,** yet his days shall be a hundred and twenty years." God's Spirit was striving with every sinner, and living in every saint, then as now. It was by this Spirit that Enoch walked with God until he was not, for God took him. It was by this Spirit that Christ spoke through all the prophets, and by it He came so near every soul that "In all their afflictions, he was afflicted, and he bare them and carried them all the days of old." Since man needed a Saviour, the river of life has been flowing from the throne of God.

Ezekiel tells us of this river of life, that the "waters issued out from under the threshold of the house eastward," and again, "they issued out of the Sanctuary." Then he seeks to give us some idea of the vastness of the river:

"And when the man that had the line in his hand went forth eastward, he measured a thousand cubits, and he brought me through the waters, the waters were to the ankles... Again he measured a thousand and brought me through, the waters were to the loins. Afterwards he measured a thousand; and it was a river that **I could not pass** over; for the waters were risen, **waters to swim** in, a river that **could not be passed over**."—Ezekiel 47:3-5.

Every swimmer knows that learning to swim is simply to trust the water. It is just like this to trust Christ, the living water. Go back with me in memory, when you first began to learn to swim. How very timid when you first went into the water only ankle deep; then another day to the knees; and then you went still farther and the water reached to the loins; and one daring day you threw yourself into the water but kept one toe on the bottom. But there came a wonderful day in your experience when you lifted your toe off the bottom and found the water would hold you up. You had learned to trust the water and swim out into the deep. O friends, praise the Lord, "waters to swim in, a river that could not be passed over!"

"There's a wideness in God's mercy,
Like the wideness of the sea."

How many Christians there are who are starving, woebegone and sad; and it is because they trust to man to feed them, and to pleasure them. But strike out into the water. Know God for yourself. Get into the primary circuit and this promise of the text is yours: "abundantly satisfied with the fatness of Thy house." Why will you not come to "the fountain of life;" and why having once known it, do you forsake it?

"Be astonished, O ye heavens, at this, and be horribly afraid, be ye very desolate, saith the Lord. For my people have committed two evils; they have forsaken me, the Fountain of Living Waters, and have hewed them out cisterns, **broken cisterns** that can hold no water."[11]

---

11 Jer. 2:12,13.

God is an inexhaustible fountain, a river that can not be passed over. There is no fathoming His love or His truth, and we never can exhaust the power of His endless life. But no wonder God says, "Be astonished, O ye heavens, at this." Men have ever been wont to go only a little way into the knowledge of God; and then, in the pride of their souls, they write out their creed and forsake the **fountain** for that **leaky cistern.**

You say, who would exchange a fountain for a cistern? A fountain gives fresh, cool water all the time, gushing up from the limitless depths, and flowing full and free. A cistern, on the contrary, only professes to hold just what is put into it, but it is worse than that; they exchange the fountain for a **leaky** cistern.

Every church has written out its creed just for these reasons: First, they claim to have the truth; and secondly, they formally, systematically stated this truth in order to hold it fast, and so transmit it to their children. In other words, they forsook and taught their children to forsake the fountain. They gave them, instead, the cistern, the creed, which they thought would hold just what they put into it.

But every creed has been a **leaky cistern.** The churches are far from having the spiritual truth and power which was ushered in by the Reformation, and much of the living water that brought new life to the world under Wesley and Whitefield has been lost. What the churches need, and we as individuals, is to forsake the creeds, leave the **leaky** cisterns, take our toes off the bottom, and strike out by faith into the "waters to swim in, a river that can not be passed over."

"Dig channels for the streams of love
Where they may broadly run,
And Love has overflowing streams
To fill them every one.

"But if at any time thou cease
Such channels to provide,
The very Fount of Love for thee
Shall soon be parched and dried.

"For we must give, if we would keep
That good thing from above;
Ceasing to give, we cease to have—
Such is the law of Love."

III

The Christian a Source of Water

"For ye are a living, divine sanctuary, as God hath said, I will dwell in them, and walk in them."—2 Corinthians 6:16. Modern English Translation.

"Know ye not that ye are the temple of God, and that the Spirit of God dwelleth in you?" For *"ye are God's building."*—1 Corinthians 3:9,16.

"In the last day, that great day of the feast, Jesus stood and cried, saying, If any man thirst, let him come to Me and drink. He that believeth on Me, as the Scripture hath said, out of him shall flow rivers of living water. But this spake He of the Spirit which they that believe on Him should receive."—John 7:37,38.

"If thou knewest the gift of God, and who it is that saith to thee, Give me to drink, thou wouldst have asked of Him, and He would have given thee the living water." "The woman said unto Him, Sir, thou hast nothing to draw with, and the well is deep; from whence then hast thou this living water?"

"Jesus answered and said unto her, whosoever drinketh of this water shall thirst again, but whosoever drinketh of the water that I shall give him shall never thirst; but the water that I shall give him shall be in him a well of water springing up into everlasting life."—John 4:10-14.

III
The Christian a Source of Water

EVERY sanctified soul is a sanctuary of God's indwelling, and wherever God has a sanctuary, the living waters issue out. Referring to the texts just quoted you will see that the believer in Christ is a **source** of this living water, so we shall not be surprised to learn that different sources of water illustrate different kinds of Christians.

In some of the western states they have what are called sinkholes. There is a fracture in the underlying strata, the rains having washed the soil down through it until a funnel-shaped depression is made. Later more rain washes down more soil and the hole at the bottom is plugged so to speak and the depression comes to hold water. **But it only holds what is put into it.** Even that slowly evaporates by the heat of the sun, or becomes green and fetid. No one would think of using such water and even the presence of the sink-hole on the farm is liable to be a source of disease.

The church today has many such Christians. The only water they ever had was collected from the shower that brought them into the church years ago. Even that has been slowly evaporating and becoming less and less. What a life to live! When the Living Fountain of the water of life is flowing fresh and free and for them, if they will but wash and drink and live. God has fresh water from the Rock each day for each one of us. When Israel was in the wilderness God fed them each day with manna from heaven. That was to show how He wants always to feed His children. Christ said, "I am that bread that came down from heaven."

You will recall that this bread would not keep over night; it bred worms. Why was this? God could have made it keep a week. In fact that which came on Friday did keep over the Sabbath; but that which came on any other day would not even keep over night. This shows clearly that God was trying to teach us all a lesson. It is that **God has fresh bread for us each day.** He does not want us to eat the stale bread of yesterday. Yet thousands of people are trying to live and even trying to feed others on bread that came forty years ago. No wonder it is mouldy.

Why did Jesus teach us to pray, "Give us **this day our daily bread**"? Why not pray "Give us this day bread for a week"? Because Jesus knew we would be trusting the bread and worshipping the bread instead of the giver. He knew that before the week was up we would even forget that He gave it to us and would think we had earned it ourselves. Ah, no! The prayer of faith is as the Master taught: "Give us this day our **daily** bread." If we believe He supplies our need today, and if we truly trust Him today, we will not worry about the morrow. He can feed us tomorrow too. It is "daily bread" now as of old, fresh bread from heaven each day.

Many a one has backslidden from God worrying over not having strength enough now to stand the seven last plagues. You have no promise of either strength or bread for tomorrow. "As thy **day** so shall thy strength be." "Therefore do not be anxious about tomorrow, for tomorrow will bring its own anxieties. Every day has trouble enough of its own."[12] God grant us bread from heaven, and water from the Rock each day, and may we walk with Him daily, and not be sink-hole Christians.

WELL CHRISTIANS

In the olden days in order to secure good, clear water, a hole was dug in the ground until a vein of water was tapped coming from some underground spring. Then it was walled up with stone or brick and a curb built around it, and a well-sweep or windlass was arranged to draw the water. How cool and sweet and refreshing the water from "the old oaken bucket" tasted.

The only trouble with this well was that it was dependent largely upon the local showers that came from the secondary circuit. If it rained every little while the water in the well was deep and clear and sweet, but if the showers failed to come for a month or six weeks the water began to get low and became roiled and ere long the well went dry.

You can see how many Christians are like that well. If they have the privilege of attending regular Sabbath meetings or revival services anywhere that "trees of righteousness" overflowing with showers of blessings abound, these Christians have water in their wells, good water, too—water of life. Often they are earnest workers for a time and rejoice in giving the living water to others who are thirsty. O yes, they are far ahead of the sink-hole type, but still they are only in the secondary circuit and utterly dependent upon the local showers

---

12 Matthew 6:34. 20th Century Version.

of blessings that come from the trees of righteousness. Let them be denied the association with other Christians for any reason and they soon lose their enthusiasm and the water gets low, and then turbid, mixed with all sorts of worldly sediment, and soon their well goes dry.

O friends, do you not know that God has something far better than that for you?

Artesian Christians

Underneath the earth's surface are different strata of rocks arranged one above another and often running unbroken for hundreds of miles. Some of these strata are pervious to water, and some are impervious. Perhaps there may be a pervious stratum between two impervious strata; and these will extend for hundreds of miles, and curve upward into mountains much too far away for us to see. There, in the upper impervious stratum, is what geologists call a "fault," so that the water from some clear mountain lake gets down through that upper stratum and then runs down through the pervious stratum, between the two impervious ones, creating a constant water pressure all along the hundreds of miles that these strata extend.

Then a hole is drilled thousands of feet, to and through the upper impervious stratum, and taps that pressure. The water comes flowing up clear, cool and constant. It is not dependent in the slightest upon local rains, and long continued local drought has no effect upon it. It comes from the inexhaustible fountains away up in the invisible hills of God.

Refer to the text at the beginning of this chapter where Jesus is speaking to the woman at the well. He would give her **living water,** and he that drinketh of this water shall **never thirst.** Dear reader, that is a flowing well. That is an artesian Christian. No more muddy water, no more dry times, no terrible thirst and unsatisfied longings. "They shall be abundantly satisfied with the fatness of thy house; and thou shalt make them drink of the river of thy pleasure; for with thee is the fountain of life." That is growing into the primary circuit. Enjoy the revival services, enjoy the assembling of yourselves together, yes, more than ever. **But we are not dependent upon them,** nor upon the local showers, for we have tapped the inexhaustible fountain away in the invisible hills of God. Jesus said it was possible for us here, and is it not worth while?

Years ago I crossed what was then the great American desert. Much of it is fertile, tillable land now. All it needed was the water of life. But then we rode hundreds of miles with nothing but blue sky over head, and sand and a little sage brush, and now and then a jackrabbit below. After what seemed like interminable hours we came into a little town by the name of Humbolt. What a transformation! Everywhere was beauty and bloom and verdure. I concluded the desert was past. After remaining only a few minutes, the train pulled out, and we were in the desert again. I asked what was the cause of all the beauty and bloom in the heart of the desert and was informed, "They have one of those **flowing wells** there." Would you not like to be able to go out into the desert and waste places of life and have verdure and bloom and beauty spring up all around you? The land before you like a wilderness and after you like the garden of the Lord?

"My soul longeth, yea, even fainteth for the courts of the Lord; my heart and my flesh crieth out for the living God. Yea, the sparrow hath found an house, and the swallow a nest for herself where she may lay her young, even thine altars, O Lord of Hosts, my King, and my God."

The soul, without God, is like a sparrow alone, without a mate, and without a house; it is like a swallow without a nest, or place for her young, but when the soul finds God, and gets into the primary circuit of blessings, then "the sparrow has found a house for herself, and the swallow a nest where she may lay her young."

"Blessed are they that DWELL in thy house; they will be still praising thee. Blessed is the man whose strength is in thee; in whose heart are the highways to Zion. Who **passing through the valley** of **Baca,** make it a **well,** [the original word is fountain] the rain also filleth the pools. They go from strength to strength, every one of them appeareth before God."[13]

The word "Baca" means "dry valley of weeping." The Targum renders it Ge-Hinnom or Gehenna, the word translated "hell." The scripture, therefore, seems to say that no place in the universe can be so bad but that the man who knows God for himself, if compelled to go to that place, can take God's Spirit with him there; and this Spirit not only will keep him sweet and beautiful, but will overflow in spiritual life and blessing all around him. As Whittier says, "Better fire-walled hell, with Thee, than golden-gated Paradise without Thee."

What a picture of the man who knows God for himself and has found in God his soul's home, and working place, and resting place. As Jesus said, "Out of him shall flow rivers of living water... and he shall never thirst again, but the water that I shall give him shall be **in him** a fountain of water springing up into **everlasting life.**"

One more scripture, the climax of all this wonderful truth of the River of God.

"A **garden enclosed** is my sister my spouse; a **spring shut up** a **fountain sealed.**"[14]

Why did God enclose that garden? Why did He shut up the spring and seal the fountain? Then the thought came to me, What comes to an unfenced garden, to a fountain whose waters are open and unprotected? You can not say to God, "I can not have fragrant,

---

13 Psalm 84:2-7. Revised Version.
14 Song of Solomon 4:12.

beautiful plants in my spiritual garden for people will trample over them and spoil them." You can not say to Him, "I can not have sweet water in my heart's fountain, for evil people come in and foul it." No, for God has promised to enclose the garden and seal up the fountain. He says, "I will watch it every moment; I will keep it night and day, lest any hurt it." And "He that keepeth Israel shall neither slumber nor sleep."

Let us read the thirteenth verse of the fourth chapter of the Song of Solomon: "Thy plants are an orchard of pomegranates, with pleasant fruits; camphire, with spikenard, spikenard and saffron; calamus and cinnamon, with all trees of frankincense; myrrh and aloes, with all the chief spices; a fountain of gardens, a well of living waters, and streams from Lebanon."

Is that not a wonderful picture of the soul saved and watered and made fragrant and beautiful by God Himself? Every plant mentioned is a fragrant plant, and, as if that were not enough, it adds "all the chief spices." O friends, let us hope and pray that our lives may be made beautiful and fragrant like that.

You ask, "If it is all enclosed and shut up and sealed, what good will the fragrance do?" Listen, now, to the last verse of this fourth chapter: "Awake, O north wind: and come, thou south; **blow upon my garden, that the spices thereof may flow out.**" The wind as well as the water is a symbol of the Spirit. The original words for "wind" and "spirit" are the same.

What a wonderful salvation! God, through Christ by the Holy Spirit, sends us the living water from His own great heart of love. He finds us dry and dead, a part of the desert world. He saves us and grows us into a beautiful living garden filled with all fragrant flowers and fruits; he fences us in and cares for us and makes our own hearts fountains of the same sweet water that flows from His throne, and then, having made us thus beautiful and fragrant, He blows over us by

His Spirit, that the fragrance and the beauty may flow out to others. Surely after this, we will ever confess Christ and say, "Not unto us, not unto us, O Lord, but to thine own name give glory."

The water of life is thus the outflowing, outreaching heart of God, through Christ, by the omnipresent Holy Spirit, seeking admission into every soul. "Whosoever will may come and take of the water of life freely." And wherever a soul receives salvation from the wonderful inflowing of this water of life and of love and of power that flows from God, that soul itself becomes a fountain, outflowing with the same saving, loving, life-giving water.

Through crucifixion with Christ we become broken and emptied of self, that the resurrection life and power, the living water, may fill us and flood us and outflow from us to the desert world around us.

"Emptied, that He might fill me, as forth in His service I go;

Broken, that so, unhindered, His love through me might flow."

"He that planteth a tree is a servant of God,
He provideth a kindness for many generations,
And faces that he hath not seen shall bless him."
—Van Dyke.

IV

The Tree of Life

"Now when I had turned, behold, at the bank of the river were very many trees on the one side and on the other."

"And by the river upon the bank thereof, on this side and on that side, shall grow all trees for meat, whose leaf shall not fade, neither shall the fruit thereof be consumed; it shall bring forth new fruit according to his months, because their waters they issued out of the sanctuary; and the fruit thereof shall be for meat, and the leaf thereof for medicine."—Ezekiel 47:7,12.

"Blessed is the man that walketh not in the counsel of the ungodly, nor standeth in the way of sinners, nor sitteth in the seat of the scornful. But his delight is in the law of the Lord; and in His law doth he meditate day and night. And he shall be like a tree planted by the rivers of water, that bringeth forth his fruit in his season; his leaf also shall not wither, and whatsoever he doeth shall prosper. The ungodly are not so; but are like the chaff which the wind driveth away."—Psalm 1:1-4.

"Thus saith the Lord; Cursed be the man that trusteth in man, and maketh flesh his arm, and whose heart departeth from the Lord. For he shall be like the heat in the desert, and shall not see when good cometh; but shall inhabit the parched places in the wilderness, in a salt land and not inhabited."—Jeremiah 17:5,6.

"Blessed is the man that trusteth in the Lord and whose hope the Lord is. For he shall be as a tree planted by the waters, and that spreadeth out her roots by the river, and shall not see when heat cometh, but her leaf shall be green and shall not be careful in the year of drought, neither shall cease from yielding fruit."—Jeremiah 17:7,8.

IV
The Tree of Life

HERE Ezekiel speaks of "very many trees," and **"all trees** for meat," growing by the bank of the river, and, if the river is a river of spiritual life and power, none other than the given life of God in Christ, what are these trees that are rooted into this water, and that are living by its life? The answer is plain. The trees rooted in the water are Christians who are in the "primary circuit," who know God for themselves, and who live their spiritual life by His life.

In the recorded words of Jesus we have another figure closely related to this, which teaches the same truth. "I am the vine, ye are the branches; he that abideth in me, and I in him, the same bringeth forth much fruit; **for without me ye can do nothing.**" We must be rooted in the divine given life and abide in it, or rather in Him, so that His life flows through us; only thus can we live spiritually and bear fruit. This figure goes through the whole Bible, teaching ever this same great truth.

We find it in the first Psalm, **"Blessed** is the man that walketh not in the counsel of the ungodly... He shall be like a **tree** planted,...

bringing forth fruit in his season." The prophet Jeremiah is even more explicit: "**Cursed** be the man that trusteth in **man**." This does not simply mean the man who trusts in man for temporal needs, but it means the man who is only in the "secondary circuit," and who, therefore, trusts **only in man** for spiritual needs. Things may go all right with him for a time, but there will surely come a dry time, when all human aid fails him.

Notice now the contrast: "**Blessed** is the man that **trusteth** in the **Lord**, and whose **hope** the **Lord is**." He shall be as a tree planted by the waters, when heat cometh the leaves shall not dry up, and in drought shall cease not from yielding fruit. What a wonderful description of the man who is rooted in the river of life that flows from the throne of God. For him there is no dry time. Even in the year of "drought," when for others everything withers and dies, he does not even have to be careful of the water supply. What prodigality of blessings!

Once I was on the very highest foothill in the whole Rocky Mountain range, and it was the dry season. For the most part the prairies were yellow and sear, but you could trace the irrigating ditches as far as the eye could reach by the greenness along their banks. Just so even the world can trace the Christian who is really rooted in God. Isaiah calls such Christians "trees of righteousness, the **planting of the Lord,** that He might be glorified."

All through the Bible **righteousness** and **life** are coupled together, even as are **sin** and **death.** They are related as cause and effect and are almost interchangeable terms. If a Christian, rooted in the fountain of unfailing water, is a tree of righteousness, he is also a **tree** of **life.** Solomon tells us, "The fruit of the righteous **is a tree** of **life**." Now God has ordained that every living thing on every plane shall bear fruit "after his kind." If, therefore, the fruit of the righteous is a tree of life, the righteous man, himself, is a **tree** of **life** to bear such fruit.

THE SIGNIFICANCE OF THIS SYMBOL

God's picture of the true man, the Christ man, is not a "bruised reed," that can not stand alone; not a "reed shaken in the wind" and yielding to every breath of temptation; but a great, splendid tree, with roots reaching down deep into the sub-soil of truth until they find the everlasting waters; and branches spreading wide to feel the spirit breath of the breezes, a tree aquiver with life in every twig and leaf while breasting the storms, and bracing itself to stand unharmed against even the sweep of the tempest. Who would not be that "noblest work of God," such a man as this?

But the **ruin** of such a tree is simply a **heap** of **ashes**. How many men there are whose lives are failures and but the ruin of what should have been grand and splendid, bound and held captive by an evil heredity and evil habits. The spirit at times futilely seeks to break the bonds and soar to utmost heights, but they are in fact **heaps** of **ashes,** when God intended they should be splendid trees.

"The Spirit of the Lord God is upon me because the Lord hath anointed me to proclaim liberty to the captives, and to say to all such, God will still give you the **beauty** for the **ashes,** that you may be called trees of righteousness, the planting of the Lord, that He might be glorified." Is not this indeed the gospel, the joyful news, the "good tidings" to "bind up the broken-hearted" and "to comfort all that mourn," and to "give unto them the oil of joy for mourning, and the garment of praise for the spirit of heaviness"?[15]

The leaves are the lungs of the tree. On the upper surface of the leaf the cells are arranged compactly so that the sun can not too easily and rapidly evaporate the moisture and wither the leaf. But on the under side, the cells are thrown loosely together, and there are

---

15 Isaiah 61:1-3.

millions of little openings or breathing pores through which the air enters freely and circulates among these cells.

In a previous chapter we noticed how the roots of a tree divide and subdivide into millions of rootlets terminating in little living microscopic sponges to take up the moisture. It is this living water, the symbol of the Spirit, thus taken up by these rootlets, that enables the tree to **appropriate** both from the **soil** and from the **air** all the elements **necessary** for **its growth**. As long as the tree continues to live, fifty, a hundred, or, in the case of the giant Sequoia, several thousand years, it constantly increases this power of **appropriation** both from the earth and from the air. Each season it spreads its roots a little wider and thrusts them down a little deeper into the moist earth.

Each year the branches grow a little longer and the leaves are increased in number, and so present more absorbing surface to the air, which, all through the Bible, is also a symbol of the Spirit. Instead of being easily satisfied, the tree, like the living thing it is, seems ever more and more to realize its utter dependence upon the air and the water, and to reach out with ever-increasing eagerness, both above and below, for these two elements of life, both of them symbols of the divine Spirit.

And what is the result to the tree? It continues to grow as long as it continues to live. Each year it makes more growth than it did the year before. Cut down any healthy tree, no matter how large or how old, and you will find the concentric circles, that show each year's growth, have not decreased in thickness as the tree has grown larger, and, as they have increased in length with the enlarging circumference of the tree, it means that each year of its life the tree has made a larger and ever larger growth.

What a wonderful lesson is here for Christians! The church is full of those who repented years ago and received forgiveness and joined the assembly of believers, and who ever since have felt that was all that was necessary, and that they had through tickets for glory. They **began** to **live** and **began** to **grow** and then stopped, and have ever since been a dead weight on the real church of God. Others have felt the inadequacy of such a limited experience of just repentance and forgiveness, and they look for a **second blessing,** which they call sanctification, expecting it to be instantaneous, like the experience of forgiveness.

I would not say anything against a **second blessing** or a **thirty-second blessing,** but, since we would be trees of righteousness, why can we not learn the lesson of the tree? Does not the Master tell us, "Blessed are they which do hunger and thirst after righteousness"? Why do we not constantly realize more and more our need of God and with ever increasing eagerness reach deeper and higher and wider the appropriating arms of our faith for the Holy Spirit's blessings? If we do this, we too, like the tree, will continue to grow more; and, since God is infinite, and there are no limitations to Him, and no limitations to man's possibilities in Him, this growth beginning here with the eternal life, will go over into the everlasting years.

It is this water of life that turns every experience that comes to the tree into a blessing. Here are two trees, one on the right hand and one on the left. You may think of them as maple trees. Everything that comes to this tree on the left seems to work together for evil. The rains rot it, the sun withers it and dries it up, and the winds break it down and leave it in ruins.

Now the tree on the right is entirely different. The rains freshen it and make it grow more rapidly; the sun warms it into a new and more vigorous life; even the tempests seem to test and strengthen the fiber of the limbs and the trunk and cause the roots to spread wider to brace the tree and reach down deeper into the soil until they tap the everlasting sources of moisture and of life.

Why is it that the same things that work for evil to one tree all work together for good to the other? What is the essential difference between these two maple trees? The one on the right has in it the water of life and is alive; while the one on the left is dead. It is this life that turns everything that is a curse to one tree into a blessing to the other.

Here are two individuals in contrast, the extremes of their kind. One we call a misanthropist, a man-hater. He thinks evil of everyone, distrusts them, and no doubt would criticize and condemn the Lord if He were here today. The other we call a philanthropist, a lover of mankind, who thinks no evil and sees good in everyone. To such a one all persons love to go in sorrow, because they are sure to receive sympathy and help. Neither of these persons has had easy paths before him. Both have had pleasure and pain, joy and sorrow, materials out of which characters are built. Why such different results in the two?

It is the same as that of the two trees. One of them was rooted in Christ, the living water, and had the spiritual life of God rooted in the life so that it transformed every curse into a blessing and made "all things work together for good." The other, lacking this life, found all things working against him. Under the same experiences of trial and disappointment he grew critical and distrustful of all mankind. Wonderful, indeed, is the transforming, glorifying power of the divine life in the soul!

Again the tree does not appropriate all these elements from the soil and air selfishly and live for self only. We have already seen how the leaves of the tree exhale moisture into the air which comes down in showers of blessings again and again.

We want to remember, also, that we are considering a fruit tree, one that is not affected by drought but yields its fruit every month, one constant round of beauty, bloom, and fruitage. Our Father made the beauty of the blossom for the eye, the fragrance of the blossom for our sense of smell, and the flavor of the fruit to appeal to the taste. Surely we can see it was His love that made and mated all these things to give His children pleasure. What a love story about our Father a beautiful fruit tree is!

And so it is with Christians who are really "trees of righteousness"; they do not appropriate the spiritual gifts of God selfishly and live for self, either for the here or for the hereafter. Their lives are fragrant, fruit-bearing lives that glorify the earth and make all around them better and happier; constantly, though perhaps unconsciously, giving to all new revelations of the Father's love.

*"Dear Lord and Master of us all,
Whate'er our name or sign,
We own Thy sway, we hear Thy call,
We test our lives by Thine."*
—Whittier.

V
Unity of Life

"In the midst of the street of it, and on either side of the river, was there the tree of life, which bare twelve manner of fruits, and yielded her fruit every month; and the leaves of the tree were for the healing of the nations."—Revelation 22:2.

"For as the body is one, and hath many members, and all the members of that one body, being many, are one body; SO ALSO IS CHRIST. For *by one Spirit are we all baptized into one body, whether we be Jews or Gentiles, whether we be bond or free; and have been all made to drink into one Spirit."*—1 Corinthians 12:12,13.

"For this cause I bow my knees unto the Father of our Lord Jesus Christ, of whom the whole family in heaven and in earth is named."—Ephesians 3:14,15.

"That in the dispensation of the fullness of time he might gather together in one all things in Christ, both which are in Heaven, and which are on earth, even in him in whom also we have obtained an inheritance."—Ephesians 1:10.

"Sanctify them through thy truth, thy word is truth... Neither pray I for these alone, but for them also which shall believe on me through their word; that they all may be one; as thou Father art in me, and I in thee, that they also may be one in us; that the world may believe that thou hast sent me."—John 17:17,20,21.

O
Unity of Life

WE WANT to consider the significance of the change of number from the plural of Ezekiel's "very many trees" and "all trees for meat" to the singular number of John's description in Revelation of "the tree of life on either side of the river." In a sense the Bible is a progressive revelation. That last sacred evening in the upper room Jesus said unto His disciples, "I have many things to say unto you, but ye can not bear them now." But He added, "I will give unto you the Spirit of truth and when He is come, He will guide you into all truth, for He shall take of the things of mine, and shall show them unto you."

This is a revelation of God's constant attitude toward us. He ever has many things to say unto us, which we, in our narrowness and bigotry, are not yet able to bear. Only as we are able to bear them does His Holy Spirit reveal them unto us. This is the reason the Bible is a progressive unfolding of "the mystery of Christ, which in other ages was not made known unto the sons of men, as it is now revealed unto His holy apostles and prophets, by the Spirit."

Long after Ezekiel and before John wrote the Revelation, Paul gave us the wonderful words of my text, "For as the body is one... so also is Christ... For this cause I bow my knees unto the Father of our Lord Jesus Christ of whom the whole family in heaven and in earth is named." Think of it, one family in heaven and in earth. And that there may be no mistaking this thought, in another place he says that we shall be gathered together in **one**. Jesus, also, prayed first for the disciples and then for us all where He says, "Sanctify them through thy truth... **that they all may be one... that they all may be one in us."**

After this wonderful prayer of Christ, and Paul had seen the many members united by **one Spirit, into one body,** what wonder that John, the beloved disciple, the one who drank most deeply of the love spirit of the Master, should see the "very many trees" of Ezekiel, united by the common life of the living water that coursed through them all, in the tree of life, the wonderful divine organism of the true church of the living God.

In the banyan tree of India we have in nature a perfect illustration of this biblical figure of many trees in one. The Standard Dictionary, twentieth century edition, describes this tree as follows: "An East-Indian tree which sends down from its branches roots that ultimately develop into accessory trunks, producing a cluster or grove of connected trunks often covering several acres,"

"Arched like the banyan o'er its pillared props."

What a picture is this of the church of Christ as He intended it to be in this age! Jesus, when here, was as dependent upon God as we are. I hear Him say, "I can of mine own self do nothing; the Father that dwelleth in me, He doeth the works." Jesus, therefore, is the original trunk, rooted into the everlasting water; and every Christian is rooted with Him into the same source of life, and united with Him through the same Spirit, by faith, into the unity for which He prayed, "that they all **may be one**... that they may be **one in us.**"

Jesus used one expression that shows us clearly that He had in His mind this same image and illustration of His church, that He saw how far the Jewish church was from realizing the picture, and that it was about to depart still farther from God until the tree became spiritually dead and dry. When they were leading Jesus forth to crucifixion, there followed Him a great company of people and of women weeping and lamenting Him, but Jesus turning unto them said, "Daughters of Jerusalem, weep not for me, but for yourselves and for your children... for if they do these things in a green tree, what shall be done in the dry?"[16] That is, if the church does this evil to me while there is still some of the living water of the Holy Spirit circulating through it, what will it not do to you when the Spirit is entirely grieved away, and the church is spiritually dead and dry?

This prayer of Christ for perfect unity will be answered. This dream of Christ will come true. This prophecy of the Holy Spirit of the living composite tree, the divine organism of the true church, will be fulfilled.

When Solomon built the temple, the workmen went into the forests and quarries and hewed out timbers and stones so perfectly according to the pattern given by the Spirit, that they came together in the perfect structure of the completed temple without the sound of axe or hammer or of any tool of iron.

The multitudinous sects of a much divided Christendom are the forests, and the world itself is the quarry where the Holy Spirit is now hewing out the material for the spiritual temple that Christ is building. The material thus prepared, as in the figure of old, will be separated from its present environment and brought together into the perfected spiritual temple, that Christ, when He comes, may "present

---

16 Luke 23:27-31.

it to Himself a glorious church, not having spot or wrinkle, or any such thing; but that it should be holy and without blemish."

Even now, in all the various sects, wherever you find true Christians, they are infinitely more at one with each other than they are with the ecclesiasticism of which they now form a part. As their spiritual growth and development continue, they will more and more realize their separation from the merely human, and their unity in the divine and spiritual church.

There is in nature a unity of life by the water, and all life is impossible without it. Scientists are coming to realize the unity of all life also. And if this unity of life is true of trees and all vegetation, so it is of the spiritual life and the spiritual trees. "By **one Spirit** ye are baptized into **one body**." Again Paul says, "For ye are **all** one in Christ Jesus." And this is true just to the degree that we are in Christ. The different sects are so many barriers that men have uplifted between human hearts to make one feel he is less our brother than another, but there is that in the triumphant Christ Spirit, even now, which will transcend them all and make us realize our essential unity with all of every nation and every sect who really know and love the Lord.

Is it not time for us to think of those who love the Lord as Christians, our full spiritual brothers and sisters in Christ Jesus? This is only possible in the Spirit and as we are divested of carnality. Nothing is more natural than for the carnal man to think of his nation and his people as superior to all others. If we have eyes to see, there is no such thing as an uninteresting face. Every face carries its life record of joy and sorrow, hope and disappointment, comedy and tragedy; but the record is written in the hieroglyphics of the heart, and, in this commercial age, that language is becoming an unknown tongue.

Years ago, all over Assyria and Babylonia, there were queer carvings on the stones, not a character or letter was known, and our history of those centuries then was mostly mythical. Max Muller and other Orientalists began with what may be called a method of scientific guessing, and they gradually reproduced the alphabet, then the grammar and the language itself. And from the translation of those cuneiform inscriptions the history of those countries has been rewritten until we seem much nearer to them, nearer than to many peoples who lived only a few centuries ago. There is need for some new Max Muller of the heart to teach us to understand and interpret these records on the faces of the people around us and bring us nearer together.

A part of the inspired description of the closing of this age, just before us, is, "Then they that feared the Lord spake **often** one to another; and the Lord hearkened, and heard it, and a book of remembrance was written before Him for them that feared the Lord, and thought upon His name. And they shall be mine, said the Lord of Hosts, in that day when I make up my jewels, and I will spare them as a man spareth his own son that serveth him."

Which means that they will no longer be strangers to each other, carrying each his own burden of trial and sorrow without the other knowing or being able to understand. The divine, unifying Spirit will have brought them nearer each other and will have so quickened their intuitions as to enable them to understand and speak the sympathetic, comforting word in season.

"There is a scene where spirits blend,
Where friend holds fellowship with friend;
Though sundered far, by faith they meet,
Around one common mercy-seat."

VI

Fellowship of Life

"There is neither Jew nor Greek, there is neither bond nor free, there is neither male nor female; for ye are all one in Christ Jesus."—Galatians 3:28.

"If we walk in the light, as He is in the light we have fellowship one with another."

—1 John 1:7.

09
Fellowship of Life

HAVE you ever seen two trees that, standing originally several feet apart, have grown together and become one? Each tree put out a limb that approached the other until finally they came together. As the wind swayed the trees, they rubbed together and irritated each other, and you might have heard a groaning, complaining sound issuing from them, but one still day, when they had pressed hard, each on the other, the sap went over from one to the other, and there was an interchange of the living fluid that from that time on grew them together.

Thus it will be, and the time is soon coming, when God's children, already hewn timbers and polished stones by the working of His Spirit, and yet still held apart by the different sects and creeds, will hear the divine Spirit saying, "Come out of her, my people, that ye be not partaker of her sins, and that ye receive not of her plagues" Then these prepared timbers and stones, these separated, consecrated souls, "fitly joined together and compacted by that which every joint supplieth, will be built upon the foundation of the apostles and prophets, Jesus Christ Himself, the chief corner stone; in whom all the building fitly framed together groweth into a holy temple in the Lord; in whom we, also, shall be builded **together** for an habitation of God, by the Spirit." The "very many trees" of Ezekiel will become "the tree of life" of John. "That in the dispensation of the fullness of time He may gather **together in one all things in Christ,** in whom we also have obtained an inheritance."

And shall we not all earnestly pray God to hasten the day when the prayer of Christ for spiritual unity and perfect fellowship may be thus answered; when, transcending all wireless telegraphy and telephony, all Spirit-taught souls may be united into perfect understanding and conscious unity by the living, pulsating current of the divine Spirit, until they "may be able to comprehend with all saints what is the breadth and length and depth and height; and to know the love of Christ, which passeth knowledge, that they may be filled with all the fullness of God."

Ezekiel also tells us, "The leaf shall not fade, neither shall the fruit thereof be consumed; it shall bring forth new fruit according to his months, because their waters they issued out of the sanctuary."

John tells us, "The tree bare twelve manner of fruits, and yielded her fruit every month." What are these fruits of the tree of life? We have seen that the water is the divine Spirit and life given by God, in Christ. "They drank of that spiritual Rock that went with them, and that Rock was Christ." We have seen that the trees are Christians in the primary circuit, rooted in Christ, and living by His life; and we have also seen that "the tree" means these same Christians unified by the Spirit into the one divine organism of the spiritual church and all rooted in this same living water of the Spirit.

Then the fruits the tree bears are "the fruits of the Spirit." We have Christ's own words, "Abide in me and I in you; as the branch can not bear fruit of itself except it abide in the vine; no more can ye except ye abide in me. If a man **abide not in me,** he is cast forth as a branch and **is withered** and men gather them, and cast them into the fire, and they are burned. Herein is my Father glorified, that **ye bear much fruit, so shall ye be my disciples."**[17]

The fruit that grows as a result of the life coursing through a peach or an apple tree, is the natural expression of the life, and is called a peach or an apple. Even so the fruits that grow as a result of the divine life, the divine Spirit, coursing through us who are living members of His body—these fruits are the natural expression of His Spirit, and are called "the fruits of the Spirit."

Paul tells us these fruits are "love, joy, peace, longsuffering, gentleness, goodness, faith, meekness, temperance; against such there is no law." Peter adds to these courage, knowledge, and patience completing the "twelve manner of fruits," and these last, equally with the others, can be shown by the scriptures to be fruits of the Spirit.

How difficult it would be to manufacture peaches and place them on a tree so they would look and taste natural. And yet it is not difficult for a living peach tree, rooted in the water, to bear peaches. Even so, how impossible it is for us to manufacture these fruits of the Spirit. What wonder that all **our** righteousness is as "filthy rags" compared with His righteousness, the "white robes," and the "wedding garment." But if we are rooted in Him and abide in Him and His life abides in us, how natural and beautiful for that divine life within us to express itself in these fruits of the Spirit.

We can not say that it is impossible for us to live consecrated lives and bear these fruits of the Spirit because the times and our environment are unfavorable. God is the only environment we need. For him who is a living tree, rooted in the everlasting fountain of life, there will come no dry time because he shall "not be careful even in the year of drought, neither shall cease from yielding fruit."

---

17 John 15:4-8.

The fruit of any plant is that which if planted will produce that plant. Scientifically speaking the real fruit of the apple is the seed. It is only commercially that we speak of the edible part that contains the seed as the fruit. These fruits of the Spirit, then, these fruits of the tree of life, are the seeds we sow if we would grow other living Christians. If you would raise real Christians, sow love, joy, patience, faith, courage, and peace.

Your own heart may be bruised and bleeding from the roughness of the world, and you may often weep in secret, but the sowing of these precious seeds, that shall be watered by the Spirit, will ultimately bring a harvest that will not only make glad the world but will also bring peace and rest to the heart of the sower. "He that goeth forth and weepeth, bearing precious seed, shall doubtless come again with rejoicing, bringing his sheaves."

John also tells us, "The leaves of the tree were for the healing of the nations," and Ezekiel says, "The leaf thereof was for medicine," or as the marginal translation reads "for bruises and sores." In the natural world the leaves of the trees exhale moisture thus creating a secondary circuit of the waters, making fruitful much land that might be barren desert. Even so in the spiritual world, the "trees of righteousness" are the cause of many a "shower of blessings" that brings God to the consciousness of many souls who might never know Him. Thus the leaves of the tree are for the healing of the nations.

When a boy in the old Granite State I often went barefoot among the stones and rocks getting bruises and sores on my feet, and I would then take leaves from some plant to bind them on the sore spots. The world is full of people with sore spots, but they are not all on their feet, mostly in their hearts, and, if we are Christians, wherever we find the sore spot, we seek to heal it and thus "bind up the broken-hearted and bring comfort to all who mourn." How shall we do it? Christ was "the Word of God," and the Bible is "the Word of

God." Christ was the "Word made flesh." He was **the** tree of life, and the Bible is a tree of life. Every promise of the blessed Word is a **leaf** off the tree of life.

Just as Jesus was a tree of life when here, and the "Word was made flesh" in His experience, so we, as we experience the promises of the divine Word in our own soul, become "the word made flesh" and the tree of life. The precious promises of God will then be the healing leaves growing on our own life tree. Then we can go to any one with a sore spot on his heart, with some of the leaves from our own life's experience all bruised and tender and cooling, and we will comfort him with the comfort wherewith God has comforted us and trust God for the healing power of love, love that breaks all barriers of creed or sect, and transcends all human limitations, love that does not even ask who is to blame but only "Wilt thou be made whole?" We pray God to fill us with such love, for it is the love of God.

*"Tis Thine to cleanse the heart,
To sanctify the soul,
To pour fresh life in every part,
And new-create the whole."*

VII

The Cleansing Blood of Christ

"The blood of Jesus Christ His Son cleanseth us from all sin."—1 John 1:7.

"For there are three who bear witness, the Spirit, and the water, and the blood, and the three agree in one."—1 John 5:8. Revised Version.

VII
The Cleansing Blood of Christ

IN ALL our study we have been discovering that the Bible is, indeed, the Book of books. If you seek depths of philosophy, exploring the inmost secret motives of human action, it is here. All the transcendentalism of the philosophers can not equal it. If you search for poetic expression, what literature can equal or surpass the Psalms of David, the Book of Job, the Prophecy of Isaiah, or the Prayer of Habakkuk?

If you desire spiritual uplifting, transforming power, it is here— the power that transformed the shepherd boy, David, into the soldier, the musician, the poet, and the king; the power that transformed Saul the bigot, into Paul the apostle; the power that enabled Jesus, though tempted in all points as we are, to live a sinless life, making Him the supreme pattern of perfection for all ages and all lands.

We have also been discovering how inadequate and arbitrary are many of the concepts that are popularly taught concerning it, and in nothing is this more true than in the teaching of the blood of Christ. The paganizing of Christianity in the great apostasy in the early ages of the church's history brought in a heathen concept of the character of God and a heathen idea of sacrifice, applying it to the sacrifice on the cross. This corrupted and transformed the whole idea of atonement and of mediation.

In this transformation, the wonderful scriptural doctrine of the blood as the given, consecrated life—a doctrine that runs like a scarlet thread of light through the whole Bible—was lost; and in its place there came the pagan idea of the literal blood, flowing to appease the wrath of God.

In this view, the blood of Christ means the death of Christ, a death made necessary by the demand of the Father for satisfaction for the sin of man. Man sinning deserved death. Before God could admit him to pardon and salvation, we are told, His wrath must be appeased, or His sense of justice must be satisfied. So Christ died, shed His blood, **in the place of man.** All who accept this death by faith as for them are admitted to pardon and then, by some divine casuistry, are accounted pure and free from sin, or let off from the damnation that was their due. Unhesitatingly, we pronounce this whole concept false, unscriptural, and unlike God.

How could God show His justice by killing the innocent for the guilty? It is no answer to say that Christ willingly gave His life. By willingly offering His life Christ showed Himself free from the selfishness that caused men to sin, and so least worthy to die of all God's creatures. And the more the love of Christ is revealed in His willingness to die, the more unlovely does God appear in demanding such a sacrifice.

For illustration, here is a family of twelve boys, and all but one are criminals, deserving to die under the law. This one is a model citizen and has always lived a loving, useful life. He offers himself to be electrocuted or hanged **in the place** of his **eleven brothers.** Would any judge consider that proposition? Of course he would not.

But suppose such a judge could be found. Would the people of this or any other community submit to such a court proceeding? Would they consider that it magnified the dignity and justice of the law and the justice of the court? No! They would think it a monstrous injustice, revolting to the heart of every honest man.

And yet, just this, which common sense knows to be unjust and unreasonable and against every man's inner sense of right, theology asks us to believe in as the one thing that magnifies the justice and the mercy of God and of His law and government. What wonder that unbelievers sneer at such teaching!

But if, instead of God damning man because he transgressed an arbitrary law, and then letting him off because Christ paid the price—if, instead of this, man doomed and damned himself by placing himself in discordance with the very principles of happiness and life, and if God, seeing man in the current of sin, going helplessly down to death, instead of demanding a price, united with Christ in making the necessary sacrifice most dear to His heart, and so paid the price Himself, reaching out through Christ after fallen man, to save him from the result of his own sin; then truly we can see the character of God revealed, a character of justice and of mercy and of infinite, pitying, Fatherly love. The whole law and government of God is then magnified and stands out, as it is in deed and in fact, as a law of love and a government of love, resting on no arbitrary fiat or decrees but on the eternal and unchanging principles of happiness and life.

In this latter case, however, the blood does not mean **death, a death demanded,** but it means **life,** a life **given** to come into our lives and save us from sin and transform us into the image and likeness of God. Does the text say that the blood of Christ, as it was shed two thousand years ago, by some mysterious, incantatory power so changed things then that all who had believed, did or should believe on Him, and accept Him as a substitute, should be admitted to pardon and then accounted pure and free from sin?

Neither; but, on the contrary, this scripture clearly speaks of a **present active power, working in man, under definite given conditions,** not to change God or His attitude toward man, but to change man and his attitude toward God, by cleansing him from sin and transforming him into the likeness of God. **"If we walk in the light, as He** is in the light." That is the given condition, a yielding of our minds and wills to God, a God who, He has just told us, "is light," and in whom "is no darkness at all." If we meet these conditions, yielding our minds and our wills to God, "the blood of Christ cleanseth," or better still, "is cleansing us from all sin," and so is bringing us into fellowship with God and each other.

Satan has sought to steal away that real, present, living spiritual fact and leave only a magic charm process, a mere accounting or letting off in the place of it.

What does the blood mean? Do not misunderstand; we wish to speak very reverently here. There is no question as to the supreme importance of the blood of Christ. All the scriptures agree that only through the blood is there forgiveness, salvation, sanctification, glorification, and complete redemption.

Ask the heroic men and noble women of every age, those of whom the world was not worthy, how they resisted evil and arose above their age into such heights and glories of moral and spiritual efflorescence, and they will say, "It was only by the blood of Christ." Ask the man who has struggled for years with temptation, struggled and failed, and has fallen in the deepest discouragement and despondency, but who has now found freedom and joy and hope for the future, what brought him to this wonderful change, and he will tell you, "It was the blood of Christ."

Ask the ones who were raised from the dead with Jesus and taken home with Him as the first fruits of them that slept, sacred band of the immortals, celestial bodyguard of the empire of mankind, how they triumphed over sin and death into the fullness of glorious life, and they will tell you, "Only by the blood of Christ." Ask the final company of the redeemed gathered out of every nation, kindred, and tongue, what brought them home, and they all with one accord cast their crowns at the feet of Christ and say, "Thou art worthy, for thou wast slain and hast redeemed us by Thy blood."

But the sacredness and the importance of the subject make us all the more want to understand what is meant by the "blood." It is written of the innumerable company of the redeemed that they "have washed their garments, and made them white in the blood of the Lamb." Literal blood would not be a means of washing anything white. Moreover, we know that these are not literal garments referred to here. It is a figure of speech, and it is not irreverent to seek to understand what it is.

The instant we deny this is a figure and consider the blood as literal, that instant we localize the action of the blood at Calvary. For we do not have the literal blood now. The blood shed on Calvary perished, like other blood. To obviate this difficulty the Roman Church has appropriated from heathenism the perpetual sacrifice of the mass, in which her priests are supposed, by means of a Latin incantation, to create the body, blood, and divinity of Christ, and so have it on hand for present use. After having, by one magic process, created the body and the blood, they offer it up, that by means of another magic process it may do its work.

Any one who knows what heathenism was will at once recognize the heathen nature and origin of the whole magic charm process. Protestantism does recognize it and repudiates it. But repudiating this, if Protestantism holds to the literal blood, she has only the local sacrifice. And when we localize the sacrifice, and therefore the action of the blood, we change the whole Bible thought of salvation by the blood of Christ into an arbitrary concept that is also heathen in its nature and origin.

If damnation is an arbitrary doom pronounced by an arbitrary God, because man transgressed an arbitrary law, and if salvation means man's escape from that arbitrary doom, because God's wrath has been appeased by the flowing blood of a propitiatory victim, then it is clear how the blood, all at once, on Calvary, could accomplish this for the whole world.

But this is neither the damnation nor the salvation that the Bible was given to reveal. The thoughtful reader of the Bible discovers that God's law is not arbitrary but a wise, loving statement of the very underlying principles of happiness and life. Man, by transgressing this law, notwithstanding the unchanging love of his Father-God, inevitably damned himself, and transgression, "sin, when it is finished, bringeth forth death."

The salvation of the Bible is salvation from sin. "His name shall be called Jesus [Saviour], for He shall save His people **from their sins.**" Now salvation from sin is a personal, individual thing, and, if the blood of Christ is the means of this salvation, it must be omnipresent and continuous in its action; it must act when and where the man is who needs salvation. This is exactly as the Bible speaks of the blood, as a present, active force, working in us, under definite given conditions, when we accept Christ by faith, to purge us and cleanse us from all sin and to change us into the divine image.

"Not all the blood of beasts,
On Jewish altars slain,
Could give the guilty conscience peace,
Or wash away the stain.

"But Christ, the heavenly Lamb,
Takes all our sins away;
A sacrifice of nobler name,
And richer blood than they."

VIII

The Blood Is the Life

"For the life of the flesh is the blood; and I have given it to you upon the altar to make an atonement for your souls; for it is the blood that maketh an atonement for the soul.

"Therefore I said unto the children of Israel, no soul of you shall eat the blood. He shall pour out the blood thereof, and cover it with dust.

"For it is the life of all flesh; the blood of it is for the life thereof; therefore I said unto the children of Israel, Ye shall eat the blood of no manner of flesh; for the life of all flesh is the blood thereof; whosoever eateth of it shall be cut off."—Leviticus 17:11-14.

VIII
The Blood Is the Life

THE blood of Christ is the omnipresent given life of Christ. As the law interprets the law, this is the significance of the blood throughout the Old Testament and in all the sacrifices. The blood is the life. We are first told this in Genesis, the ninth chapter, and fourth verse, "But flesh with the life thereof, which is the blood thereof, shall ye not eat."

By referring to my texts you will see the law is interpreting itself. As the sacrifice, or offering, represented the person who brought it, so the blood of the sacrifice represented the life of the one who sacrificed. Or, as no man can truly bring himself to God and consecrate himself, but only does this as Christ lives in him and controls his life by His divine indwelling life; **so the blood of the sacrifice represented the blood of Christ, in the man, bringing him to God.**

The shedding of the blood was the giving of the life. The shed blood was the **given life.** The consecrated blood, with the flesh, in the "whole burnt offering," consuming on the altar of burnt offering, by the sacred fire which God had kindled, coming up as a sweet odor to God, represented the consecrated life, given and consumed in His service. Eating the blood represented saving the life or appropriating the life to self, and "whosoever saveth his life shall lose it. Whosoever eateth the blood shall die."

In the New Testament it is the same. When the soldier pierced the side of the crucified Christ on the cross, there came therefrom two streams, one of blood and one of water. Do these two streams mean death to appease the wrath of God or to pay the price He has demanded? Or do they mean life, the **given life** of God in Christ? "For there are three who bear witness, the Spirit, the water, and the blood, and the three agree in one." Here, then, is the test. Do these three, which all agree in one, all mean death? Or do they all mean the **given life?**

Does the Spirit mean death? Never. It is the very source and essence of **life.** The second verse in the Bible tells us that the Spirit moved upon or brooded over the chaos, to create and make alive. "Thou sendest forth Thy Spirit, they are created: and thou renewest the face of the earth." Jesus said, "The words that I speak unto you are Spirit and **life.**" The very word for Spirit, in the New Testament, is also translated "life," but never death or anything associated with death.

Does the water mean death, or does it mean life? All through the Bible the river of life flowing from the throne of God is the symbol of the given Spirit or life of God. The water is called "the water of life." It is always the very antithesis of death. Jesus said, "The water which I shall give you shall be in you a fountain of water **springing up into everlasting life.**"

And the Spirit and the water and the blood, as John tells us, agree. "The blood is the life;" "The blood is for the life;" "The blood is all one with the life." Thus the Bible agrees that the three mean life, not death. The blood of Christ is, therefore, the life of Christ, and the life of God given us in and through Christ is for our salvation from sin. The scriptures never speak of the blood as of a price paid **to the**

Father for our pardon, or of the blood of Christ as having some merit in the Father's sight, which propitiates Him and causes Him to let us off.

Instead of this, the Spirit, the water, and the blood, all three of which agree in one, are always spoken of as the outreaching or outflowing of the Father's heart, through Christ, to reach His wandering children and bring them to repentance, forgiveness, and salvation from sin, and so back into harmony with Himself and with the heavenly family.

Do you ask when this blood or this divine life was given to save us from sin and from death? We answer Christ is a "lamb slain from the foundation of the world." The gift of the Spirit was in the gift of the Son. It was then the living rock was smitten, and ever since the living water of life has been flowing from the throne and from the heart of God, coming so near every one that whosoever will may take thereof and **live.**

God revealed this omnipresent, given, saving life in many ways: in the bush that burned and was not consumed; in the water from the rock; in the bread from heaven; in the sanctuary and the offerings, and in Aaron's rod that budded and bore fruit. Most of all He revealed it in the men and women who were lifted above their hard and sordid surroundings, and were saved and transformed and glorified by the indwelling Spirit—men and women pilgrims and strangers, hated and persecuted by the world, who out of weakness were made strong, sanctified, and some of them even translated, by the blood of Christ or by this given life.

Notwithstanding all these revelations and manifestations of this omnipresent, given, saving life, still men lost this living, spiritual truth out of all these revelations and had only the cold and lifeless forms left. Then the incarnate Christ came, and by His life and death revealed all over again this one saving fact of the omnipresent, given, outflowing, saving divine life. He not only revealed it, but in His own life He demonstrated the all-sufficiency of its power to enable one tempted in all points as we are to live without sin and find salvation, glorification, resurrection, and even translation.

Remember "the blood is the life," and Jesus said, **"I am come that ye might have life, and have it more abundantly."** It may be difficult to define life, but this we do know, it is the power to act. An active person we call a lively person. Physical life is the power to act physically, and spiritual life is the power to act spiritually, in harmony with the spiritual law.

Paul recognized this fact and knew that spiritual life was the one thing needed for our salvation when he said, "If there had been a **law** given which **could have given life,** verily righteousness should have been by the law." If the law could have imparted the power to keep the law, salvation could have come by the law.

Those who teach that God demanded a price before He would admit man to pardon and salvation, need to consider and remember this fact. Over and over again the Bible says of God's laws, "He that doeth them shall live in them." And Jesus assented to this and said, "This do, and thou shalt live." The only reason, therefore, why men can not gain salvation out of the law, under the old covenant, without Christ, is because they have not the spiritual life to keep the spiritual law, and the law itself **can not impart this life.**

Paul says, "What the law could not do, in that it was weak through the flesh," God sent His Son to do, for "the law of the Spirit of life in Christ Jesus, hath made us free from the law of sin and death," "that the righteousness of the law might be fulfilled in us, who walk not after the flesh, but after the Spirit."[18] Christ then, came to give us His blood, or His spiritual life. He said, Except ye eat my flesh and drink my blood, ye have **no life in you.** Notice that His blood was not

---

18 Romans 8:1-4.

to appease the Father or to pay the price to God, but it was **to impart life to us.** "And this is the record," says John, "that God hath given to us **eternal life,** and this life is in His Son. He that hath the Son **hath life;** and he that **hath not the Son of God hath not life."**

By this same given life of God, Jesus' life was made perfect and beautiful, "not after a law of carnal commandments, but after the **power of an endless life."** And Jesus said, "He that believeth on the Son **hath everlasting life,** and he that believeth not the Son, shall not see life." And again, "Verily, verily, I say unto you, He that heareth my word, and believeth on Him that sent me, **hath everlasting life,** and shall not come into condemnation; but is passed from death unto life."[19] It can not be denied that this means **salvation through the imparted spiritual life of God in Christ.** But salvation is by the blood of Christ, so here, too, **the blood** is seen to be **the life.**

The Bible teaches this same truth in many ways. Christ says, "Abide in me... As the branch can not bear fruit except it abide in the vine, no more can ye except ye abide in me." The branch, by abiding in the vine, **receives of the blood, or life of the vine,** and so is enabled to live and bear fruit. And so Jesus says, "I am the vine, ye are the branches." Could anything teach more clearly that **we are saved** and are to **live spiritually** and bear fruit **by His blood,** or **by His imparted spiritual life?**

You will recall the Psalmist says of God, "With Thee is the fountain of life." The shed blood of Christ is, therefore, a figure of the outflowing life of God, for Jesus said, "He that hath seen me, hath seen the Father." This outflowing life of God is omnipresent in Christ, by the Spirit, knocking at the door of every heart, seeking to come in and abide there, bringing salvation.

---

19 John 5:24.

Remember that the Spirit, the water, and the blood all "agree in one," and they proceed from and represent alike the Father and the Son; for of the one who yields his heart fully to this cleansing blood, Jesus says, "We will come unto him and make **our abode** with him."

*"Jesus, Thy blood and righteousness
My beauty are, my glorious dress;
Mid flaming worlds in these arrayed,
With joy shall I lift up my head."*

IX

The Symbol of the Blood

"Except ye eat the flesh of the Son of man, and drink His blood, ye have no life in you."

—John 6:53.

IX
The Symbol of the Blood

THE Bible is a revelation from the known to the unknown, from the physical to the spiritual. Its figures are borrowed from the visible physical world but are used to teach spiritual lessons. This figure of the blood is no exception. To understand it, we need first to know what the physical blood does in these bodies of ours.

The work of the blood in the body is twofold: (1) to cleanse and (2) to feed and repair, to build up and cause us to grow. The blood is constantly cleansing our bodies from poisons. It takes these poisons around to the lungs, where they are thrown off through our breath; it takes them to the skin, where they are sent out through the pores. It sends them to the kidney, the liver, and the intestines and to every excretive eliminative organ of the body.

In throwing out these impurities, the blood does not consider what we may believe to be impure or poisonous, but it acts according to the divine laws which are often entirely beyond our knowledge. We may think tobacco is good and take it into our mouth, but the blood knows it is not, and it rushes to the glands of the cheeks and makes the saliva flow to wash it away. We may think whiskey is good and drink it, but the blood instantly recognizes it as a poison and rushes it to the lungs and to the pores of the skin to throw it off as soon as possible.

This cleansing, purifying work on the spiritual plane is the first work of Christ's blood in us. "The blood of Jesus Christ His Son cleanseth us from **all sin.**" Not merely from what we may think or believe to be sin, but from **all sin.** The inspired writer of the Book of Hebrews, after speaking of the blood of bulls and goats, says, "How much more shall the blood of Christ, who through the eternal Spirit offered Himself without spot to God, purge your conscience from **dead** works to serve the **living God.**"

Please notice in these two texts that the blood does not represent a substitutionary, propitiatory death, a price paid to the Father years ago, once for all. It represents a **living, present, active power,** working in the believer. We may think our works are good. Abraham did and longed that he and his people might live before God, but the blood of Christ in us knows that our works are of the flesh and so purges them out. It purges our conscience, too, so that we may see the things of the flesh are not of God.

When the innumerable company of the saved speak of having "washed their robes and made them white in the blood of the lamb," they refer to this cleansing, purging power of the blood of Christ, seeking out all the evils in our characters, the ones we do not know as well as those we do know, removing them, and leaving our robes of character without spot. This is the work of the blood or life of Christ in us, to search us and know us and reveal us unto ourselves and to will in us and work through this willing to purify us. It is thus that men are redeemed from sin and brought back to God by the blood of Christ.

The second work of the physical blood in the body is to feed the body, thus repairing its waste and causing it to grow. In this feeding process, the blood absorbs the nutriment from the digested food and carries it throughout the entire body, distributing to each organ and part exactly what is there needed for repair and for work and growth. This is a fact so wonderful as to show divine intelligence even in the physical blood of the body. The parts of the body are exceedingly varied in their nature and requirements. The liver cells need one kind of food and the kidney cells another kind. The needs of the muscles and of the nerves are different each from the other and widely different from those of the liver and kidneys. And so with every part of the body, from the fluids to the solid enamel of the teeth. But the same blood, circulating through them all, with superhuman intelligence separates from itself and supplies to each exactly what is needed and nothing else and then goes on its way. These needs of the body differ each day and at different times in the same day, but all these differing needs are fully considered and accurately met by the circulating blood of the healthy human body.

Christ said, "I am that living bread… My flesh is meat indeed, and my blood is drink indeed… Except ye eat the flesh of the Son of man and drink His blood, ye have **no life** in you." Thus the blood of Christ, the life of Christ, the divine Spirit, for all three agree in one, circulating through His body, the church, brings to each member of that body exactly what is needed and at just the right time. We are to take no anxious thought for the morrow. God, who clothes the lilies, will clothe us with spiritual beauty. God, who feeds the ravens and the sparrows, will feed us with heavenly bread. Oh, the joy of it!

The physical blood, in feeding the body, develops us, not into an image we may choose for ourselves, but into an image chosen before of God, through the divine law of heredity, the image of our physical parents. We may greatly desire to have blue eyes and grow to be six feet tall, "but which of you by taking thought can add one cubit unto his stature?" It is the same in the spiritual realm with the blood of Christ. It develops us into the divinely appointed image, the pattern of heavenly things, the image of our Father. "Now the God of peace,... through the blood of the everlasting covenant, **make you perfect** in every good work to do His will, **working in you** that which is well-pleasing in His sight, through Jesus Christ; to whom be glory for ever and ever."

From these texts you will clearly see that the blood of Christ, instead of representing a death paid once for all, as a price to the Father, when Jesus died on Calvary, represents the omnipresent spiritual presence and life of the Father and Son, a means by which God, through Christ, reaches out after men, bringing them to repentance and pardon, purging, washing, and cleansing them, and then changing them into the realization of God's perfect ideal for them.

The blood of Christ does in us spiritually exactly what the physical blood does in us physically. The figure here, as in many cases in the Bible, is a carrying of the physical laws into the spiritual realm, a using of the known physical to reveal the unknown spiritual. Some may say the circulation of the blood was not known until the time of Servetus or Harvey. God knew it, and the Bible was written for all time. The learning of the world never outgrows the Bible. Besides men even then did know that the **blood represented the life,** and that it was life in us that eliminated poisons and developed us hereditarily into the image of our parents.

In perfect health our own blood perfectly cleanses the body from all poisons, known and unknown; but in many forms of ill health blood loses its power to do this work, the blood itself becomes weak and lacking in vitality, and the person affected is doomed unless there is aid from without.

Under these circumstances, if the invalid has a healthy friend who is willing to allow the surgeon to tap the arteries and transfuse healthy blood into the weakened circulation of the patient, the friend actually gives life and vital energy to the invalid, in the giving of the blood. This transfused, healthy blood immediately begins to work in the unhealthy body to purge out the poisons and to restore health.

Transfusion of blood is a fact, demonstrated scientifically, and has already saved many lives. We all live by the life of God. "In Him we live and move and have our being." The life of God imparted in creation, and through the creative processes, was sufficient to bring man into the perfect realization of God's thought physically and spiritually.

But man sinned and came short of the glory of God. Through sin the law of heredity, which was ordained only unto life, began to work in part unto death. Through transgression of the law of happiness and life man brought upon himself physical and spiritual sickness and death, thus damning and dooming himself. Because of this he is spiritually weak, alienated from the life of God, and anemic and thus unable to cleanse and purify himself and grow into the divine ideal.

God, the fountain of life, through Christ, in the new birth, imparts His life, transfuses His blood, making us branches of the **living** vine; so that the divine life blood may course through us, cleansing us and changing us, through a new heredity, "the law of the spirit of life in Christ Jesus," into His own image, and making us bear the fruit of His Spirit. This is salvation. **We are saved by transfusion of blood, but it is a spiritual transfusion, as it is a spiritual salvation,** and a spiritual and eternal life.

"Greater love hath no man than this, that he lay down his life for a friend… But God commendeth His love for us in that, while we were yet enemies, Christ died for us." But when, through His given life, we are brought to repentance and pardon and open our hearts to the cleansing flood of His eternal life, we are no more strangers or foreigners, nor are we servants, merely, but Christ says, **"I have called you friends; for all things that I have heard of my Father I have made known unto you."**

This intimate relationship of God through Christ is wonderful. We are to eat His flesh and drink His blood, else we have **no life** in us. **It is a continuous transfusion, a constant flowing of His life into us,** of the sap of the vine, flowing through the branches. It is a coming of both the Father and the Son into our lives to make their abode with us. It is Christ living with us, and in us, on such terms of intimate friendship that He and His Father have no secrets that they hold from us; but all things that Christ learns from the Father, He makes known to us as soon as we are able to bear them. "Thus we walk in the light as He is in the light," and the constant inflowing divine life cleanseth us from all sin.

John, in holy vision, saw the innumerable company of those thus cleansed, and he heard the question, "What are these which are arrayed in white robes and whence came they?" Then came the answer, "These are they which came out of great tribulation, and have washed their robes and made them white in the blood of the Lamb; therefore are they before the throne of God and serve Him day and night in His temple; and He that sitteth on the throne shall dwell in them. They shall hunger no more, neither thirst any more, for the Lamb which is in the midst of the throne shall feed them, and shall lead them unto living fountains of waters; and God shall wipe away all tears from their eyes."[20]

---

20 Revelation 7:13-17.

*"My hope is built on nothing less
Than Jesus' blood and righteousness;
I dare not trust the sweetest frame,
But wholly lean on Jesus' name.
On Christ, the solid Rock, I stand,
All other ground is sinking sand."*

X

Two Kinds of Righteousness

"But we are all as an unclean thing, and all our righteousnesses are as filthy rags."

—Isaiah 64:6.

"I will greatly rejoice in the Lord, my soul shall be joyful in my God; for He *hath clothed me with the garments of salvation,* He *hath covered me with the robe of righteousness, as a bridegroom decketh himself with ornaments, and as a bride adorneth herself with her jewels."*—Isaiah 61:10.

X
Two Kinds of Righteousness

THE great lesson of the previous chapter being that of our absolute dependence upon the indwelling life of Christ for any fruits of righteousness to appear in our lives, we shall proceed now to consider under a different symbol frequently used in the scriptures.

Of the two kinds of righteousness spoken of in the Bible, one is called "our righteousness," "self-righteousness," and "the righteousness of the Pharisees." All these are the righteousness of the old covenant, the righteousness of human effort and of ambitious striving after goodness. The other kind of righteousness is called "God's righteousness," "Christ's righteousness," and the "righteousness of the saints." These three are one, the righteousness of the new covenant and of the divine, indwelling life.

For these two kinds of righteousness there are running through the entire Bible two sets of symbols. Our righteousness or self-righteousness is called "filthy rags," "filthy garments," and an "unclean thing." God's righteousness or Christ's righteousness is called "the fine linen," "white robes," "the wedding garment," "the garment of salvation," "the robe of righteousness," "the breastplate of righteousness," "the jeweled robe," and "the holy garments."

These two kinds of righteousness are as entirely different as are the symbols God has chosen to represent them. The more we have of "our righteousness," or "self-righteousness," the more critical and condemnatory we are, and the more inclined we are to disagree with those who do not see all things exactly as we do. But the more we have of "God's righteousness," or "Christ's righteousness," the broader and sweeter we are, the freer we are from all criticism, and the more we are able, like God, to love men who are even dead in trespasses and sin; and the more we are able, like Jesus, to open our arms wide and take all humanity to our hearts, humanity with its sufferings and its sins, with its weaknesses, its failures, longings, and aspirations.

Just as there are two kinds of righteousness spoken of in the Bible, so there are two ways of seeking righteousness described; one is by the old covenant or by works, and the other is by the new covenant or by faith. And it is plainly shown that however zealously, earnestly, or sincerely we may seek righteousness, if we seek it in the wrong way, we are sure to get the wrong kind.

Israel of old sought righteousness by the "law of righteousness," a law which is "holy and just and good," and all the commandments of which "are righteousness." Paul bears them record that they were zealous in their effort to get righteousness from this law of righteousness, and yet they reaped only the wrong kind and became Pharisees instead of true Israelites or Christians. And why? Because they, "being ignorant of the righteousness of God" which is by faith, and "going about to establish their own righteousness" by the works of the law, "have not submitted themselves unto the righteousness of God."

And all the while they were making this fatal mistake, the righteousness of God, which is by faith of Christ, was not far away from them; but Christ was knocking at the door of each heart, speaking on this wise, "Say not in thine heart, who shall ascend into Heaven, to bring Christ down? or who shall descend into the deep to bring Christ from the dead?... But the Word is nigh thee even in thy mouth and in thine heart."

If the danger of making this mistake were past and this record had for us only historical interest, I would not consider it for a moment; but the fact is that thousands of sincere people are making the same fatal mistake now and are becoming self-righteous instead of righteous.

There is nothing today so good, so essentially a part of true religion, but what, approaching it in the wrong way, through the old covenant instead of through the new, we may secure the wrong kind of righteousness out of it. Reading the Bible, keeping the Sabbath, going to church, prayer, all these are good, all are an essential part of the Christian life; and yet we may easily place all these into the old covenant and get only self-righteousness out of them.

We can readily understand this if we remember that Israel did not get her self-righteousness and Pharisaism out of some evil thing but out of zealously seeking righteousness by the law of righteousness which was holy, just, and good.

For instance, since I am a Christian I feel I **ought** to read the Bible, and I resolve to do so and to be faithful in the performance of this Christian **duty.** By reading three chapters each day and five on Sabbath I can read the Bible through in a year; so I start in determined to be faithful, and for some time I allow nothing to interfere with my daily readings. Before long I begin to watch others and feel quite sure there is no one else in the church so faithful in reading the Bible, and how easily and naturally I begin to pray the prayer of the Pharisee, "Oh, Lord, I thank thee I am not as other men; I read the Bible every day." I have placed the reading of the scripture into the old covenant and am getting only old covenant righteousness out of it.

But instead of reading the Bible from a sense of duty, I feel and know that here is spread the very table of the Lord for my soul's needs. I come to the Bible not from a sense of duty but because I am hungry and want to come, and I consider it a most blessed privilege to read God's Word. He talks to me out of His Word, my soul is fed and strengthened and filled with quiet trust and joy and with a growing sympathetic love for those who have not learned to love the Bible as I love it. This is reading the Bible in the new covenant, the Word is made flesh in our lives, and we become righteous with the righteousness of Christ.

Again I say, "I am a Christian and a member of the church, and Christians **ought** to pray." Think of it, "ought to pray." How would your dearest friend feel if he overheard you say to some one, "I think I **ought** to talk to my friend once in a while." What is prayer? It is the outreaching of the heart's longing after God. Mere words, however beautiful, are not prayer. The man who tries to pray from a sense of duty is really not praying at all but only **making a prayer.**

But, not realizing all this, I resolve to be very faithful in prayer morning, noon, and night, and inevitably before long I begin to think I am more faithful in prayer than others in the church; so I place prayer into the old covenant, and only self-righteousness results.

Instead of duty, however, you realize that prayer is the very island of the blessed, the half-way house between earth and heaven, where the Soul of the Infinite and the hungry heart of man meet, and the man finds strength and courage and companionship and a consciousness of soul-satisfying love. The man who thus, through the blessed privilege of prayer, rests in the everlasting arms and finds his feet shod with the preparation of the gospel of peace for all of life's rough pathways, receives from prayer the same comfort and righteousness that Jesus received, two thousand years ago, with communion with His Father on the hills and in the woods of Judea and Galilee. The same glow will be in his heart and on his face that the disciples recognized on the face of the Master when they said to Him, "Teach us to pray."

These two illustrations will suffice to show how every Christian's **new-covenant privilege** may be placed in the old covenant and made a duty merely and a source of "works" and of self-righteous human effort.

Jesus "abolished **in His flesh,** the law of commandments contained in ordinances." This does not mean merely an external abolition of the old ceremonial law. The very wording of the passage makes it signify an experience in the life of Christ. Another scripture speaking of Christ says, "Who is made **not after the law of a carnal commandment,** but **after the power of an endless life.**"

The two scriptures belong together in the experience of Christ. The reason He was not made after the law of a carnal commandment was because He **had abolished in His flesh** the law of commandments contained in ordinances. He had ceased to do anything from the mere external motive of **duty** or fear of blame or for the desire of approbation of men. Thus all of His outward acts had become the natural, spontaneous expression of the abiding life of God in His soul.

There has been so much Pharisaism and so little Christianity in the world, so much of the wrong kind of righteousness and so little of the true righteousness of Christ, that the very word "righteousness" has come to have a forbidding and repellent sound in the unbelieving ear.

*"Just as I am, and waiting not
To rid my soul of one dark blot,
To Thee, whose blood can cleanse each spot,
O Lamb of God, I come."*

XI

The Change of Raiment

"The fine linen is the righteousness of the saints."—Revelation 19:8.

XI
The Change of Raiment

WE SHALL seek to show from the various symbols of righteousness in the Bible that the righteousness of Christ is not the cold, formal, ceremonial thing it is thought to be, but the spiritual efflorescence of the human soul into all the beauty of tenderest love and widest, deepest sympathy and understanding.

When the Lord chooses a physical symbol to represent some spiritual fact or experience, if you study carefully the symbol, you will get a revelation of the thing symbolized.

Let us study a field of flax. It stands up straight with a beautiful blue blossom and seems to say, "Look at me; see how beautiful I am." But before the flax becomes linen, it is mowed down and laid flat on the ground until freed from all useless matter; it is then dried, and must be hatcheled until all the stiffness is gone and only the yielding fiber remains. Then, and only then, can this fiber be spun and woven into fine linen.

So it is with us starting out in life with our own aims, ambitions and purposes which seem to us beautiful and worth while. But self has to be crucified. We have to be mowed down, and hatcheled out until only the yielding fiber remains. It is the most difficult experience of all to learn that in me, that is, in my flesh, dwelleth no good thing. Even our aspirations and our prayers are selfish and imperfect.

Abraham said of Ishmael, the child of his own works, "Oh, that Ishmael might live before thee!" But God said, "Cast out the bondwoman and her son." It is the age-long struggle of humanity with God, wrought out in each human soul, "Oh, that **my** works might be received of Thee!" But as of old God says, "Cast them out."

I once saw a machine for weaving brocaded silk. It had a half dozen shuttles with different colored threads plying back and forth, working according to a set pattern, and out of this apparent confusion, growing thread by thread, without a human hand touching it, beautiful silk was woven, with leaves and flowers and fronds of ferns, showing in colored silk threads.

It is thus, when through many bitter experiences of failure and loss we finally learn to yield our fiber into the hands of the Master Workman, that God can spin and weave into our lives, according to His pattern, the **"fine linen of His righteousness."**

There is also significance in the colors. When the Bible speaks of "white robes" and the "white raiment" and "the fine linen, clean and white," we know that "white" represents purity and separation from the selfishness of the world. And we know also in this connection that colors with the "fine linen" of righteousness are significant.

In studying the "holy garments" and "jeweled robe" of the priests referred to in the text as a symbol of righteousness, we see that the colors, blue and purple and scarlet, are mentioned over and over again and always in connection with the linen. Read these scriptures, and it is not difficult to understand their meaning, that we find in Exodus 28:5, 6, 15, and 33.

When we speak of blue, the spiritual Jews understood blue to represent the heavenly source of righteousness. No earthly motive can ever produce or inspire the heavenly righteousness. The inspiration of Christ's righteousness is always that divine, self-sacrificing love that is born only from above.

Purple is the royal color. Christ is **King** of Righteousness and Prince of Peace, and His Kingdom only is eternal. The **throne** of God was in the sanctuary; but, says Paul in Second Corinthians, sixth chapter and sixteenth verse, in the Modern English Translation, "Ye are a living, divine sanctuary." God is seeking to establish His throne in each human heart and to rule supreme there. Christ said, "The kingdom of God is within you." How appropriate then the royal purple of the sanctuary and of the priestly robes. For righteousness in the human heart is the one and only infallible evidence that God, through Christ, has there established His throne. Righteousness is the true royal purple of the soul, and this kingdom within is everlasting.

Scarlet is the color of shed blood. It means sacrifice, the giving of the life. It is the very foundation of all righteousness. The righteousness or unrighteousness of each heart is determined by whether it gives or keeps the life. The life of the sinner centers in **self.** The life of the Christian, like the Master, is a given life, consecrated by love to the service of others.

"Except you take up your cross and deny yourself daily, and come after me, ye can not be my disciple."

"Whosoever saveth his life, will lose it."

"Who is this that cometh from Edom with **dyed garments** from Bozrah?"

The robe of righteousness of the Christian, even as of Christ, will show the scarlet of the shed blood of the given life.

The robe of the ephod was all blue, every thread of fine linen, woven without a seam, having an opening for the head to pass through; and the whole garment hung in graceful folds from the shoulders, reaching nearly to the feet. Around the bottom of the robe was "a bell and a pomegranate, a bell and a pomegranate round the hem of the robe to minister in." The bells were of pure gold, and the pomegranates were of blue and purple and scarlet and fine twined linen. The pomegranate was used even in the ancient mysteries as a significant fruit. (See Hislop's "Two Babylons," page 111.) It is a fruit full of seeds. It is fruit unto more fruit. So this fruit hanging on this robe represents the fruit of righteousness, the fruit of the Christ Spirit, which is "love, joy, peace, long-suffering, gentleness, goodness, faith, meekness, temperance."

You will notice this "robe" had a "bell and a pomegranate, a bell and a pomegranate," just as much fruit as profession of fruit; and the fruit is full of seeds, a fruit with the divine, living, germinal power of producing more fruit. This is the righteousness of Christ. All the great constructive forces in the universe work quietly. The oak grows silently in the forest for a hundred years; today is as yesterday. Tomorrow the woodman comes with his axe and cuts it down. The tree announces itself with a far-sounding crash only as **it falls.** Destructive forces are noisy.

We read of Christ, "He shall not strive, nor cry, nor lift up nor cause His voice to be heard in the streets." The life of Christ in us is the one great constructive, spiritual force, and it is as silent in its workings in us as was the divine life in Him. Wherever there is the tinkling bell, the golden voice of praise and thanksgiving, there is always the fruit of the Spirit manifested.

*"Called unto holiness, praise His dear name,
This blessed secret to faith now made plain,
Not our own righteousness, but Christ within,
Living and reigning and saving from sin."*

XII

The Breastplate of Righteousness

"Stand therefore, having your loins girt about with truth, and having on the breastplate of righteousness."—Ephesians 6:14.

"And thou shalt make a plate of pure gold, and grave upon it, like the engraving of a signet, 'Holiness to the Lord.' And thou shalt put it on a blue lace, that it may be upon the mitre; upon the forefront of the mitre shall it be. And it shall be upon Aaron's forehead, that Aaron may bear the iniquity of the holy things, which the children of Israel shall hallow in all their holy gifts; and it shall be always upon his forehead, that they may be accepted before the Lord."—Exodus 28:36-38.

XII

The Breastplate of Righteousness

THE breastplate worn by the high priest, who was a type of Christ, was made of all the materials which, wherever they occur in the Bible, signify righteousness. It was made of "gold tried in the fire," and of "blue and purple and scarlet and fine twined linen." It was four-square, about nine inches each way, and on it there were four rings of gold with which it was laced to the ephod. The square of the breastplate was set with twelve precious stones of as many different varieties, set in gold, in four rows, three in a row. These stones were engraved with the names of the twelve tribes of Israel, each a precious stone with the name of a tribe. In order to understand the meaning, we must first consider the significance of the precious stones and then of these tribal names.

The Precious Stones

God calls His children His "jewels," "a royal diadem," "the stones of a crown." Not only does this show how precious the children of the Lord are to Him, but there is a much deeper meaning. These redeemed souls are the trophies of Christ's love, the visible evidences of His supremacy and kingship in the kingdom of love; and so they are "as the stones of a crown, lifted up as an ensign upon His hand."

But, if possible, there is something here even more wonderful than this. What is the beauty and value of a precious stone? The beauty and value is not so manifest in the beginning. One of the most famous of precious stones, now worth millions, was unrecognized and used for months as a plaything for children in the garden of a South African home.

The cutting and polishing process that brings out the beauty and value of the stone requires months and sometimes years of skilled labor and effort. The beauty and value is not in the stone itself but in the power it has acquired, through this cutting and polishing process, of reflecting to our eyes the beauty and glory of the sunshine. The peculiar beauty of each stone is in the fact that it reflects the sunlight in a little different way from that of any other stone. This is true of the different varieties of stones, and it is also true of each specimen of the same variety.

The diamond reflects all the rays of the sunlight equally, but separates them. The ruby absorbs some of the rays but reflects a predominance of the red rays, so we see it red. The emerald reflects a predominance of the green rays, and we see it green; but the beauty of all these precious stones is not in themselves at all, but in the power they have acquired of reflecting and revealing to us the beauty of the sunlight.

So of God's precious jewels. "Not unto us, not unto us, but to Thy name give glory." The beauty of the Christian is in the power he has of reflecting and revealing the beauty of the "Sun of Righteousness." And this beauty and power came to him through the cutting and polishing process.

The great Lapidary of the universe chooses rough stones from earth's quarry, and, through many experiences of both pleasure and pain, He cuts and polishes us until each spiritual Israelite or Christian is a precious jewel, able to reveal God to men in a little different way from that of any one else in the world. When the Lord has perfected us, He will then have a perfect revelation of Himself.

THE SIGNIFICANCE OF THE NAMES

In the Bible, names represent the reality of the thing named. When Abram had a new experience, he received a new name, Abraham. When Jacob had the experience of the new birth, the Lord said to him, "Thy name shall be called no more Jacob [supplanter] but Israel [prince of God], for as a prince hast thou power with God and with men and hast prevailed." When Saul had a new experience, he received a new character; he was no longer Saul but Paul. God's name is just what God is. "The Lord passed by and proclaimed the name of the Lord: the Lord, the Lord God, merciful and gracious, longsuffering and abundant in goodness and truth."

So these twelve tribal names, cut in the twelve precious stones of the breastplate, represent all of the Israel of God. Israel is one born of the Spirit; hence only the real Israel are saved. The eternal city has twelve gates, and on these gates are the names of the twelve tribes. All who enter there go in as Israelites; for, "if ye be Christ's, then are ye Abraham's seed and heirs according to the promise." So the breastplate represents **all of God's saved children as His precious jewels.**

"And Aaron shall bear the names of the children of Israel in the breastplate… **upon his heart,** when he goeth in… before the Lord **continually.**" Oh, reader, do you see this wonderful truth? Christ, our High Priest, bears us, each one, upon **His heart** before God continually. Christ wears us, each one, as precious jewels upon **His heart,** before God. This is all shown in the breastplate, and it is the righteousness of Christ, a love that will not let us go and that can not be denied, that seeks us, lost upon the mountains, until He finds us and brings us back to the Father's house.

If this is Christ's righteousness in Him, His righteousness in us will be the same, a love that will carry the unsaved and lost upon **our hearts** and will not let them go, a love that will count them the most precious ornaments and jewels of our lives, if we can win them and bring them to God. This righteousness of Christ is the tenderest, sweetest thing on earth.

Aaron wore on his head a mitre, which was made of linen and blue lace and gold tried in the fire. What a strange expression is quoted in the text which refers to the mitre. It is said the high priest shall "**bear** the **iniquity** of the **holy things,** which the children of Israel shall hallow in all their holy gifts." The mitre worn on the head and especially the plate of pure gold worn on the forehead referred to the thoughts. The gift meant the giver, as the offering represented him who brought it. It is here represented that Christ, our High Priest, bears the **iniquity** of even our **holiest thoughts** and of our **purest aspirations.**

A good man, when presenting to God his prayers and praise, often has many vain and foolish thoughts come unbidden, as the unclean fowls came down on the sacrifices which Abraham had laid before the Lord. He asks, Can the pure God accept such impure offerings as we have brought to His altar? There is so much of self and sin in our **holiest things** that our very tears need washing, and even our repentance needs to be repented of.

The Lord has made our hearts His temple by coming into them Himself to dwell there, but His pure presence makes us more conscious of every imperfection, and we hear the great King saying, "Sanctify now yourselves and sanctify the house of the Lord God of your fathers and carry forth the filthiness out of the holy place." Christ is thus sanctifying us if we trust in Him by faith. He is carrying forth the filthiness. He even now bears the iniquity of our holy things, and so God sees us not as we are but as we are to be when Christ's work in us is done, and when we stand accepted in the Beloved.

It is as though Christ said to the Father, I know, Father, they are imperfect, and even their prayers and holiest aspirations have much of selfishness in them; but they mean them to be pure, and they are under covenant relations with Me. Trust Me "to present them faultless before the presence of Thy glory with exceeding joy." And the Father rejoices to accept us thus in Christ.

And this is the righteousness of Christ, not to judge us nor condemn, but even Himself to bear the iniquity of our holy things that we may be accepted. If this is Christ's righteousness in Him, will not Christ's righteousness in us be marked by an entire absence of the spirit of judging and condemning others? It is self-righteousness that is ever full of the spirit of condemnation.

The righteousness of Christ says, "Judge not that ye be not judged." "Therefore, thou art inexcusable, O Man, whosoever thou art that judgest, for wherein thou judgest another, thou condemnest thyself." "Who art thou that judgest another man's servant? To his own master he standeth or falleth. Yea, he shall be holden up, for God is able to make him stand."

These two kinds of righteousness that in contrast run through the whole Bible come to their culmination and climax in two classes at the last great day.

One class comes up to the gate of the eternal city with great self-assurance and says, "Lord, Lord, open unto us; have we not prophesied in Thy name, and in Thy name cast out devils, and in Thy name done many wonderful works?" But Jesus says unto them, "Depart from me, I **never knew you.**"

The other class, at that great day, who have never thought of themselves as worthy, and who make no demands, to them Jesus says, "Come, ye blessed of my Father, inherit the kingdom prepared for you from the foundation of the world. For I was an hungred, and ye gave me meat; I was thirsty, and ye gave me drink; I was a stranger, and ye took me in; naked, and ye clothed me; I was sick, and ye visited me; I was in prison, and ye came unto me.

"Then shall the righteous answer Him, saying, Lord, when saw we Thee an hungred, and fed Thee? or thirsty, and gave Thee drink? When saw we Thee a stranger, and took Thee in? or naked, and clothed Thee? Or when saw we Thee sick, or in prison, and came unto Thee? And the King shall answer,... Inasmuch as ye have done it unto one of the least of these my brethren, **ye have done it unto me.**"

Behold here in contrast the offensive self-consciousness of all self-righteousness and the beautiful unconsciousness of the righteousness of Christ.

"The King's daughter is all glorious within," and so the inner glory manifests itself in outer actions of love. Lord, make us beautiful within.

"Hush! oh, hush! for the Father hath fullness of joy in store,
Treasures of power and wisdom, and pleasures for evermore;
Blessing and honor and glory, endless, infinite bliss;
Child of His love and His choice, oh, canst thou not wait for this?"
—Havergal.

XIII

Fullness of Life in Christ

"Beware lest any man spoil you through philosophy and vain deceit, after the tradition of men, after the rudiments of the world, and not after Christ.

"For in Him dwelleth all the fullness of the Godhead bodily. And ye are complete in Him, which is the head of all principality and power."—Colossians 2:8-10.

XIII
Fullness of Life in Christ

GOD created the soul of man for Himself, and only in God can that soul realize its true destiny and find its satisfaction and rest. Since God made the soul for Himself, He is of right supreme Lord of the soul; and in this He is a jealous God, in that He would make each soul a stronghold and fortress dedicated only to Him and acknowledging no invaders or interlopers.

However, God rules the soul not arbitrarily from without, which would inevitably enslave it and dwarf and distort personality, but God rules it through Christ by love from within, thus making it absolutely free; and, by the twin processes of crucifixion and resurrection carried on in each life, He merges the Christ personality into ours and ours into His, thus developing personality to its very highest possibility.

It was for this purpose that God sent His Son into the world. "God so **loved** the world"—the cosmos. This is a familiar text, but few have understood it. We want you to understand the figure. The word cosmos means order, harmony, symmetry, and beauty. We do not know how long this world had lain desolate before God, through Christ, began to recreate it. We do know it had become empty and desolate and darkness was on the face of the deep; it had become a chaos, the opposite to cosmos.

But God saw the possibility in it and sent Christ to bring cosmos out of chaos, and under Christ's recreative touch and Word the chaos became a cosmos—a beautiful, fertile, illuminated, heaven-encompassed world. Each man is a microcosm or a little world. Through sin all of us have become out of harmony with each other and at war with ourselves, but God's keen eye of constructive, creative Love sees the possibilities of each, sees the cosmos underneath the chaos, and He sent His Son with recreative power to bring it out—that is, to bring our personality to the highest possible completeness.

This is what that familiar text says: "God so loved" the cosmos in each one of us, that He sent His only begotten Son, that whosoever believeth on Him, thus admitting Him creatively into the life, shall not come to nothing, but come to everything. "A house divided against itself can not stand." Chaos with its discord and internal strife is doomed and will ultimately perish. It is self-destructive. "Sin when it is finished bringeth forth death." But cosmos, being harmonious, constructive, progressive, can go on to the utmost possible summit of perfection; having no destructive elements, it has eternal life.

Fullness of life, perfection of personality, is therefore Christ's mission to every human soul who will admit Him and yield to Him his heart and life. How weak are all human philosophies in the presence of such a divine possibility as this! No wonder Paul cautioned the brethren to beware lest any man spoil them through philosophy and vain deceit. There have been and are many human philosophies that have had their day in seeking to satisfy the human soul, ending inevitably only in failure since God alone can satisfy.

Epicureanism taught that the supreme end of life was pleasure, happiness here. That life was the most successful which garnered the most happiness day by day. The epicure's motto was, "Let us eat, drink, and be merry, for tomorrow we die." Their definition of pleasure was "absence of pain in the body and of trouble in the soul." Their concept even of happiness, as you see by this definition, was only negative. Their weakness and failure lay in the fact that happiness is not found by seeking it but by forgetting it in service. Carlyle says, "There is a higher than happiness, which is blessedness." Their philosophy too easily degenerated into license, and, while they promised liberty, they were the servants of corruption.

Stoicism said, "Happiness is impossible here; pain and suffering are inevitable. That life is the greatest success that can come to bear these most indifferently and heroically." Heroic suffering is a goal that will never be able to satisfy the human soul. Then, too, experience has shown that he who becomes most indifferent to suffering in himself is ever most indifferent to it in others and most likely to cause it. Of the two perhaps we would prefer to live among the Epicureans rather than among the Stoics.

Plato said that neither happiness nor indifference to suffering was the true end of life, but virtue was the true quest. Everything that came to us, wealth or poverty, happiness or pain, was good or evil not in itself alone but according as it ministered or failed to minister to virtue. In order that his philosophy might have time to work itself out he assumed eternity for all. Much of so-called modern Christianity comes from Plato rather than from Christ; even as Plato's works are textbooks in many modern schools of theology where the Bible is not. Plato's weakness was in his definition of virtue, in that it was of the head rather than of the heart. It was intellectual rather than spiritual, and it lacked the supreme element, the creative Christ.

The modern philosophy which led to the World War, its motto, "Might makes right," deified brute force and overrode every sacred, loving principle of life. There are forms of religion, even of Christianity, so-called, that partake more of the nature of a philosophy than of a true religion in that their appeal is more to the head than to the heart.

Salvation is not primarily physical or intellectual; it is spiritual. It is not what I can do with my body or what I can think with my brain; it is what I am in my heart; and the heart is the seat of the affections. "He that dwelleth in love, dwelleth in God and God in Him." Jesus says, "Ye shall know the truth and the truth shall make you free." This is a wonderful statement and true on all planes. Physical truth will make you free physically; intellectual truth will make you free intellectually, but it takes spiritual truth, spiritually known, to save the soul and make one free spiritually. Jesus speaks of it on the highest plane, not of intellectually knowing a theory but of spiritually knowing a personality. This is salvation—eternal life—"that they may know Thee, the only true God, and Jesus Christ whom Thou hast sent."

No wonder Paul said, "Beware lest any man spoil you through philosophy or vain deceit" or as the Twentieth Century Version reads "a hollow sham." Philosophies may be and are good and evil. The best of them may be excellent as developers of the intellect, but, as means of salvation and of bringing the highest, the eternal completeness into the life, they are all a hollow sham and vain deceit. It is here that the good is an enemy of the best.

Satan will, if he can, keep men immersed in physical things only. Failing in this he will become an advocate of higher education, so-called, substituting higher criticism and human philosophy for God and His Word. He well knows that all the great universities of the world can do their utmost for the mind and never touch the soul of life at all. All the philosophies of the world are the width of the universe from the religion of Christ. They lack utterly the spiritual creative power. Only God can hear and answer the heart cry, "Create in me a clean heart, O God, and renew a right spirit within me." "We are His workmanship created in Christ Jesus, unto good works."

Again Paul warns us against the "rudiments of the world." While this includes the world's philosophies, it includes also something else. In the second chapter of Colossians, we have these words, "Wherefore, if ye be dead with Christ from the rudiments of the world, why as though living in the world are ye subject to ordinances… after the commandments and doctrines of men?" Ritualism and ceremonialism, the result of human doctrines and human ordinances, have ever come up in the church as spirituality has declined. They help one to feel pious after he has ceased to be so in reality. (See verse twenty-three of the same chapter.) They are the rudiments of the world. Paul points us to Christ and to Him alone as the only One who can save and make complete the soul.

Into the great conflict of the universe between right and wrong, truth and falsehood, life and death, Christ entered freely. "For the joy that was set before Him" He endured the hardship, despised the shame, was made perfect through suffering, and became the Captain of our salvation. He was able to lead us on, to succor those who are tempted, to feed the weak. He was given for a Leader and a Commander unto the people.

We all have a part with Him in this same conflict. He said, "Except ye deny yourself daily and take up your cross and come after me, ye can not be my disciple." We are unable to avoid this conflict of the ages. It comes into our own families. "A man's foes shall be they of his own household." It comes nearer than that; it comes into our own hearts and lives. "The spirit lusteth against the flesh, and the flesh against the spirit, so ye can not do the things that you would." We can not dodge it. The only question is, Shall we fight alone and fail or under a Commander who never lost a battle?

As Christianity differs from every human philosophy, so Christ differs from every human teacher, in that He addressed Himself not to the intellect *(alone)* but to the *(mind through the)* heart and the spiritual nature of man. This was because He wanted to awaken that spiritual embryo within into newness of all-controlling life.

"We are workers together with God." "The riches of the glory of this mystery is Christ in you the hope of glory." Why? "Ye have overcome... because greater is He that is in you than he that is in the world." The thought is of a real transformation through the eternal law of crucifixion and resurrection into fullness of life.

How incomplete we are without Him. Even physically there are possibilities we never realize here. So He, Christ, "shall change these vile bodies, fashioning them like unto His glorious body." There the inhabitant shall not say, "I am sick"; and "there shall be no more death, neither sorrow nor crying, neither shall there be any more pain, for the former things are passed away. And God shall wipe away all tears from their eyes." Even physically we need completeness and can find it only in Christ.

Intellectually the man most satisfied with what he knows is the man most ignorant. We never can find intellectual satisfaction here. The mountain of truth and knowledge may have its base on earth, but its summit is in heaven only. Every step we take up its rugged sides shows us a mighty expanding country hitherto unknown. We long to explore it and to solve its mysteries, but life is too short. The most eager searchers after knowledge are "Excelsiors" perishing in the snow before attaining the height of their ambition. But in Christ are all the treasures of wisdom and knowledge, all the fullness of the God-head bodily; in Him too is eternal life for "he that hath the Son hath the everlasting life." We can not measure the possibilities of intellectual completeness in Him. The very nature of the mind is such as in health and continued life to make it capable of endless progress.

And what shall we say of spiritual completeness in Christ? "It doth not yet appear what we shall be." "Eye hath not seen, ear hath not heard," but God is revealing these spiritual possibilities unto us by the Spirit, day by day.

Beloved, my heartfelt wish for you is "that Christ may dwell in your hearts by faith; that ye, being rooted and grounded in love, may be able to comprehend with all saints what is the breadth and length and depth and height; and to know the love of Christ, which passeth knowledge that ye might be filled with all the fullness of God."

"Now unto Him that is able to do exceeding abundantly above all that we ask or think, according to the power that worketh in us, unto Him be glory in the church by Christ Jesus throughout all ages, world without end. Amen." Ephesians 3:17-21.

www.ingramcontent.com/pod-product-compliance
Lightning Source LLC
LaVergne TN
LVHW041843070526
838199LV00045BA/1411